THE WALL STREET JOURNAL.

GUIDE TO STARTING FRESH

THE WALL STREET JOURNAL.

GUIDE TO STARTING FRESH

How to Leave Financial Hardships Behind
and Take Control of Your Financial Life

KAREN BLUMENTHAL

CROWN
BUSINESS
NEW YORK

Published in the United States by Crown Business, an imprint of the Crown Publishing Group, a division of Random House, Inc., New York.
www.crownpublishing.com

CROWN BUSINESS is a trademark and CROWN and the Rising Sun colophon are registered trademarks of Random House, Inc.

Crown Business books are available at special discounts for bulk purchases for sales promotions or corporate use. Special editions, including personalized covers, excerpts of existing books, or books with corporate logos, can be created in large quantities for special needs. For more information, contact Premium Sales at (212) 572-2232 or e-mail specialmarkets@randomhouse.com.

Library of Congress Cataloging-in-Publication Data

Blumenthal, Karen.
The Wall Street journal guide to starting fresh : how to leave financial hardships behind and take control of your financial life / Karen Blumenthal.—1st ed.
p. cm.
Includes bibliographical references and index.
1. Finance, Personal.   2. Debt.   I. Wall Street journal.   II. Title.
HG179.B56635 2011
332.024—dc23   2011023485

ISBN 978-0-307-58873-9
eISBN 978-0-307-58874-6

Printed in the United States of America

Book design by Mauna Eichner and Lee Fukui
Jacket illustration © Peter Hoey/TheIspot.com

10 9 8 7 6 5 4 3 2 1

First Edition

CONTENTS

THE WALL STREET JOURNAL.

GUIDE TO STARTING FRESH

INTRODUCTION

Starting over is never easy.

No matter how old you are, major life changes are scary. And it doesn't help matters that some of the scariest changes are ones that also tend to wreak havoc on your finances. This is true whether you've been blindsided by a job loss, you've experienced the death of a spouse, or you have known for some time that the day of reckoning will come, as with bankruptcy or foreclosure or divorce. A million decisions seem to be staring at you all of a sudden, demanding resolution at a time when your emotions are most frayed and vulnerable. You may feel overwhelmed, frightened, confused, or maybe even paralyzed by the enormity of the challenge ahead.

This book seeks to ease that pain and allow you to move forward by helping you get a handle on what you can control: your financial life. You rarely can choose the curveballs that life throws at you or predict the grief or emotional roller coaster that may follow. You can't help the fact that by their very nature, divorce, the death of a spouse, and the loss of a job create financial hardship. But step by step, you can make decisions about your money, your spending, and your debt that can help put you back in control and on the way to building your new financial life.

Taking a slow-and-steady approach, this guide walks you first through the issues that need immediate attention, like where to look for assistance and how to make the best use of a cash influx from a settlement, an inheritance, or a severance check. You'll get a good, clear look at how financial institutions, lenders, and credit bureaus will size you up, as well as an introduction to the new health-insurance law to ensure that you have adequate and appropriate coverage.

Because the specifics of a divorce or bankruptcy are more legal matters than financial, this guide won't advise you on how to divide property or whether a bankruptcy filing is the right decision. But once those wrenching moves are under way, it will try to help you get back on track to recovery.

As you move past the initial adjustment period, this guide addresses thornier questions: How can you adjust your budget to your new situation? Should you move or should you stay? Should you borrow to buy things or pay cash? And what kinds of insurance do you need now?

If you haven't borrowed money or applied for a new credit card in a while, you'll get up-to-date information on new rules for credit, banking, and mortgages that have been put in place since the 2008 financial crisis. And you will also find concrete and understandable advice for how to best invest and manage your retirement funds under your new circumstances.

Because there is no single way to manage money—and no one lifestyle that fits everyone—this guide will offer options to identify and set your own personal financial priorities and carry them out in a way that works for you. Not every section may apply to your situation, but there are many areas of financial life that you may not even realize need a fresh look when you are starting over.

If you've been through a significant trauma, you have a lot of healing ahead. Having a grip on your finances can soften the blow and empower you to move forward with confidence in other parts of your life. This book will help you take those first important steps.

CHAPTER 1

TAKING YOUR FIRST STEPS

As you remake your financial life, here's the first big decision you need to make: decide that you won't make any big financial decisions right away.

Not making decisions may seem as scary as trying to resolve all your problems at once. But if you're hurting or feeling wrung out or emotional, there's a good chance that you won't be making your best decisions right now. And you don't need poor choices compounding the challenges you already have.

You shouldn't have to rush into anything right away—and you should be skeptical of anyone who pushes you to make a big-ticket spending decision. Almost any financial issue that seems to be looming over your head right now will still be there when you are better ready to deal with it in the near future.

You'll make better choices and fare better down the road if you take some time to step back, reflect, assess, and get your bearings. Here are your Fresh Start First Steps.

ALLOW YOURSELF A CHANCE TO GRIEVE

It's true that you can't weep or sulk or stomp around in anger forever. But whether you've suffered the painful loss of a job, the end of a marriage, the death of a loved one, or a significant financial setback, you need to allow yourself some time to grieve. Be honest about the brute impact of the loss. Give yourself permission to be sad. If you try to steamroll ahead without any mourning time, you may be surprised at how the grief will bubble up again and knock you back when you think you are really moving forward.

So allow yourself a genuine pity party—just not a big one. This period of reflection doesn't need to be expensive or dramatic. This is not the time to console yourself with a new car or a long trip to the Caribbean or even a wardrobe overhaul— those are the kinds of big financial decisions that you agreed not to make. Rather, get together with close friends. Take a weekend trip to see a beloved family member. Choose a small extravagance—a new haircut, a massage, or a meal at a restaurant you always wanted to try.

Then, identify your first small goal: set the date when you will be ready to get back to taking care of your day-to-day business, and resolve to do your best to get going then.

REFLECT

Your next step is both harder and more rewarding: make a mental list—or a real one—of what you value most in life, even if it feels like you've lost the one thing you valued most.

The goal of this exercise, cheesy as it might seem, is to try to put your new personal and financial challenges into perspective. We spend a lot of time and effort on making money, managing money, and talking and thinking and worrying about money. But for all that attention, money isn't the reason we get up in the morning or what we look forward to on our calendars. In fact, research has shown again and again that buying things, even the best-looking shoes or the coolest new cell phones, raises our spirits for only a very short time.

Instead, our greatest sources of happiness are our personal and social relationships, and those activities that enrich us, whether they're hobbies, volunteer work, or otherwise participating in something we're passionate about. We sweat about living in the right neighborhood when what really matters is being close to the places we spend our time, like work, school, or our churches and synagogues. We obsess about the cars we drive or compare notes about the trips we take, but the enduring memories are about those people we were with and what happened when we were together.

All of this is to say that as you go through the process of sorting out your new life, you will want to put your current relationships and your personal values front and center. And your first priorities should be whatever will truly fulfill you and make you happiest as you adjust to your new situation. Once you identify what that is, it will help you make the tough choices about where your money will go.

Here's the good news: If your priority is spending time with your kids or seeing your best friend once a year or visiting family more often, those may well be accomplished on the tightest of budgets. A great time with a friend can be an old-fashioned sleepover instead of a swing through Las Vegas. An afternoon in a public park can be as satisfying as a spa weekend. And a special night with your kids can be renting a classic movie you've never seen rather than the big-budget film just opening.

Along with weighing your specific priorities for how you spend your time, ask yourself what really matters to you, what your personal values are. As you go through your day, what are the forces that motivate you? Is money one of them? If not, what factors take top billing? Faith? Achievement? Commitment? Friendship?

Ask yourself, what makes you happiest in your work? Is it the paycheck? Or is it the creativity or brainpower you contribute? The chance to climb the corporate ladder? The sense of humor of your coworkers? Is your fantasy job one that gives you prestige and authority or one that gives you lots of choice and flexibility so that you can exercise more, cook more, or simply have more free time?

You'll be wrestling with the really expensive choices later, like your retirement fund or your children's educations. But for now, you want to keep your focus on what you really care about and why. Reflect on that, daydream, and right here, make a list of the top priorities you have for your new life.

1.

2.

3.

4.

5.

These will guide you through this transition and make your most painful decisions easier to endure.

TAKE INVENTORY

Before you can make smart financial moves or decisions, you have to know where you stand financially. That means digging through the files, the stacked-up mail, and the old memory bank to figure out what you really have. Yes, it can be painful and scary, and you may want to ease into it slowly. But once you have real insight into your financial situation, you'll be in much better shape to make important decisions.

Many of us keep decent track of our checking account balance, or take at least a periodic look at our retirement or brokerage statements. But if you have had a major life change, you're going to have to take an even deeper look at your financial paperwork. If you have lost a spouse, you may need to inventory all your shared belongings, as well as your spouse's individual assets, on behalf of the estate. If you are going through a divorce, you may need to go through each and every asset in order to split it all up. If you've lost a job, it's helpful to take stock of every penny so that you can think more creatively about how to move forward. Besides, lining up and assessing all your assets can be incredibly reassuring because you often have more than you think you do.

Here's what you need to know:

- Where are your saving accounts and checking accounts and how much is in them? Are there accounts at your company credit union? Any old accounts that you never actually closed? While you're at it, do you have computer logins and passwords to all of them, so that you can check them online?

- Do you have any certificates of deposit? Money market funds? Savings bonds?

- Where are your retirement accounts, 401(k)s or 403(b)s and individual retirement accounts (IRAs or Roth IRAs)? How much is in them?

- Do you have any other brokerage accounts? Do you own any mutual funds, stocks, or bonds?

- Do you (or your spouse) have a safe-deposit box with any valuables in it? If so, where is it?

- Are there any insurance policies with a cash value? If you lost a spouse, is there life insurance that can be collected? Don't forget to check with the most recent employer: some firms include life-insurance policies in an employee's benefits plan or allow employees to buy policies with paycheck deductions. You might also check groups your spouse belonged to or car or homeowners policies to see if there is additional coverage.

- If you own your house, what's it worth? This isn't a hard and fast number, but you can look at your tax assessment or try an online service like Zillow.com, just to get an idea what the current market value might be.

- Do you own any other property, like a rental home, vacation house, office condo, or another real estate investment? If so, can you estimate its value?

- What is your car worth? You can get a pretty good idea of the market value at Kelley Blue Book (www.kbb.com), cars .com, or other car sites.

- What other assets do you have? Most household items don't have much worth, beyond their sentimental value. But do you have expensive jewelry? Fine art? A collection with some market value? A family business?

Once you have all your assets written down in one place, add it up to get an idea of what you'll have for both your current needs and your future ones. Eyeball it for where the bulk of your financial value is. Are you cash-rich or cash-poor? That is, do you have just enough cash for this week—or is cash mostly what you have? (Ideally, you'll have enough in easily accessible savings to cover at least three to six months of expenses.) Do you have mutual funds or other investments that could be easily sold in an emergency? Or is most of your money tied up in a home or car or small business, which isn't easily turned to cash? These are the pieces of your personal financial puzzle, which you can move around to help make your new lifestyle work. Understanding where they are and what they are will be crucial to helping you do just that.

Now that you've taken stock (and hopefully been pleasantly surprised by what you have), get a handle on your financial obligations:

- What do you owe on your house mortgage? Do you owe money on any other real estate investments or properties?

- What do you owe each year in property taxes? Do you have any unpaid taxes?

- Do you have a car loan or loans? How much do you owe? And is it more or less than the car is worth?

- What do you owe on each of your credit cards?

- Do you have education loans? What's the balance?

- Do you owe on medical bills? Funeral expenses?

- Do you have any other debts or major obligations?

The point of this is to get a good handle on your rough "net worth"—what you actually have minus what you owe. Add up all the things you own and subtract all your debts. Hopefully, there is a nice amount left over. If so, that's your cushion and your future. It's a number that should give you confidence that you can handle whatever new challenges come your way.

If the number is very small, or negative, then you have some financial work cut out for you. You will also know up front what your financial flexibility will be, at least until you can increase your assets or reduce your debts. But don't despair; it's not hopeless. Even if you find yourself in the red, you still have options, which will be explained throughout this book.

What's important here isn't the actual bottom line itself, but getting everything into one list. Seeing it all on paper should make your finances feel less intimidating and less complicated than they used to. And understanding your net worth will help you figure out what kinds of options you have when it comes time to make the really big decisions, like whether to move or stay put, and whether you must make big changes in your lifestyle. Before you can set new goals or identify where you want to go, you need to know where you are today.

BABY STEPS

Even while you're getting your bearings, there are a few baby steps worth taking to lay a foundation for what's to come.

If you were recently laid off. As soon as you can do it, go ahead and file for unemployment insurance with your state office. It can take three to four weeks for the first check to be paid, so you will want to get the process in gear. More details about how unemployment insurance works are in Chapter 4, "Adapting to Your New Reality."

If you recently lost a spouse. Call the Social Security office to get that application under way, especially if you have children under the age of eighteen. Social Security may be able to provide crucial income for you and your family, but accessing this resource requires a fair bit of paperwork. In addition, call the human resources department where your spouse worked; there may be benefits to help you right away. More details are in Chapter 4.

Managing a windfall. You may find yourself in this transition time with a large bundle of cash or other assets—an inheritance, severance check, life-insurance payment, or a divorce settlement—and a big itch to do something with it. But remember your pledge not to make any big decisions right away!

In most cases, that money has already been earmarked, even if you aren't aware of it. It will be crucial to your retirement, to help send your children to college, or to get you through a transition between your old life and your new one. Tempting as it might be, it isn't there for a vacation home or a big splurge on that cruise you always wanted to take. In fact, how you manage that money could well set the course for the next phase of your financial life.

For now, you need to park those dollars in a safe place that earns some kind of return. In 2011, interest rates on savings and money market accounts at banks were almost too low to measure, so there wasn't a lot of value in shopping around for the very highest rates. But bank accounts are insured by the Federal Deposit Insurance Corp. for up to $250,000 each, so that's a perfectly safe way to sock your money away. (Although it is extremely rare for depositors to lose any money in a bank account, you may want to deposit your money in two different banks if you have more than $250,000.)

Online savings accounts, like those offered by federally

insured banks like Ally Bank, DollarSavingsDirect, HSBC, and others, often pay among the industry's highest interest rates, though "high" may not seem too high today. To deposit your money in an online bank account, you will either transfer money electronically from your regular checking account to your new account or mail in a check. From then on, all your banking will be online.

For reasons that seem out of date in the modern era, it can take up to three business days to transfer money from an online savings account back to your checking account. So if you know you will need the money for a tuition payment or some other expense, you'll need to give yourself a few days to transfer the money to your regular checking account so you can get to it.

When the big windfall first comes in, you should ideally put it all away until you have a financial plan. (If you absolutely need some now, take out no more than what you need for immediate living expenses.) And please note: if the money is in a retirement plan, like a 401(k), 403(b), or IRA, don't take anything out right now. Tax rules for such withdrawals are very strict and you'll want to consider the penalties before you think about touching that money.

KEEPING YOUR HEAD UP

As overwhelmed as you might feel by the upheaval in your life, you can't completely ignore the rest of the world. You'll need to stay on top of your rent or mortgage, pay your utility bills, and address other costs of daily life. In simple terms, that means you need to be sure there is cash in your main bank account to cover living expenses while you work out your future plans.

If you are in the process of getting a divorce, financial planners say the following are the minimum resources each spouse should hope to have right off the bat—and they apply to anyone else who has suffered a setback, too. Whether you have them now or you have to build to them, these should be your financial foundation:

IF YOU ARE SUDDENLY SINGLE

If you have lost a spouse or gone through a divorce, you will need to take care of a raft of paperwork to ensure accounts are properly billed and your financial house is properly titled and in order. This process can seem endless and overwhelming, especially as you get shuttled from phone rep to phone rep or encounter a variety of confusing state regulations or estate laws.

In the case of divorce, removing one person from a loan or credit card may be tough, if not impossible to do, and you may find that the debt must be refinanced or paid off. Otherwise, you could be responsible for it if your ex doesn't pay as promised.

Before you start, you'll need a number of copies—perhaps two dozen or more—of your spouse's death certificate or of the divorce paperwork.

While these changes need to be taken care of in the weeks or maybe months after your loss, they don't have to happen all at once. Do what you can, making a call or two a day or sending a couple of e-mails or letters at a time until you have worked through the list.

To some degree, you've already got much of your to-do list once you've compiled your assets, debts, and regular bills. People who have been through this before suggest using a spiral notebook, entering each account on a page, so you can keep track of when you called, who you spoke with, and what else needs to be done. Here are many of the things you'll want to update:

- Your child's school, doctor, camp, and other records, detailing who to contact in case of an emergency

- Your own emergency contact information on file with doctors, your employer, and others

- Auto title—rules will vary by state

- Car loan

- Bank accounts

- Safe-deposit box

- Brokerage and mutual fund accounts

- Guardian accounts for children

- Credit cards (for details, see Chapter 5)

- Mortgage

- Property tax assessor-collector

- Gas and electric utilities

- Phone, cable, satellite companies, and subscription services, like Netflix

- Cell-phone contract

- Home security provider

- Airline miles

- Insurance policies

- Beneficiary for your life insurance

- Beneficiaries for your 401(k), 403(b), IRA, or other retirement accounts

- Your will and other related paperwork (see Chapter 10)

- A place to live that's safe and reasonably comfortable

- An emergency fund with enough cash (or investments that can be quickly converted to cash) to cover your minimum needs for at least three months and hopefully more

- Some money set aside for your retirement

- Health-care coverage

- Funds to help support the kids (and in the case of a death or divorce, both disability insurance and life insurance that will cover each child's support if the payer cannot work or passes away)

If you have been a careful planner all along, you'll have an emergency reserve or rainy-day fund to draw on for these immediate needs. Do a rough calculation of your bills and transfer in enough cash to last you for the next couple of months so that you aren't sweating every check you write. That should give you plenty of time to prepare for your next steps. Set aside some time every week to go through your bills and pay them; depending on the changes in your life, there may be new expenses that you aren't used to paying, with new due dates. Better yet, sign into your bank account and set up automatic payments so that you don't spend too much of your precious time writing and mailing checks.

If your situation has left you short of cash, either temporarily or long term, then you'll need to make some choices and take some action. You may feel embarrassed or shy about it, but you aren't the first person to encounter a rough patch. You'll do yourself a huge favor by being up front about the problem now rather than waiting until your bills are stacked up and creditors are barking in your ear.

If you truly cannot pay some bills or if you have already missed some payments, contact the creditors—the sooner the better—and let them know that you'll need some time to figure out your situation. Explain your problem, but be succinct; this isn't the time to unload your emotions or worries. Depending on the circumstances, the creditor may be willing to work with you on a plan or simply give you thirty or sixty days more to figure things out. Write down the name of the person you spoke with and make notes about the conversation so you can refer back to them later.

You won't get a free ride: you'll be running up interest charges and maybe penalty charges, too. It's also possible that your credit limit will be cut, meaning you won't be able to charge any more until you start paying your bills again. But talking with your creditors now may buy you time and may help you out down the road, a subject we'll cover in more depth in Chapter 5, "Getting (and Keeping) Credit."

Your main concern at the outset of a crisis or a major life transition needs to be steadying yourself and your family and coming to grips with your new situation. Then you can start to take the next step, which is figuring out who can help you rebuild your financial life.

CHAPTER 2

BUILDING YOUR TRUST TEAM

As someone who is going through a difficult and painful time, you're probably more than familiar with that old saying: in a crisis, you really learn who your friends are. No doubt, as you've gone through a job loss, personal financial setback, divorce, or death of a loved one, you've learned first-hand who shows up and who disappears, who you can call on and those to skip over.

As you begin your new financial life, you'll want to keep that same radar up and running while you consider how you want to move forward. You may find you'll need a lot of professional help—maybe a lawyer to help with an estate, a financial adviser to assist with budgeting or investments, an accountant to navigate complex tax rules, or an insurance agent to help protect you and your family in the future. Wherever you live, there are many excellent people who will truly want to help you. But there will also be a fair number of so-called professionals who may try to sell you products or services that you don't need to benefit their own bank accounts. Some of them may be quite persuasive.

One of the great challenges of coming out of a crisis is protecting yourself from people who may prey on your vulnerabilities and gaps in your knowledge while, at the same time, also building strong trusting relationships with the people who can help you relaunch your new life in the right direction. It's important to remember that the trust in these kinds of relationships works both ways: you need to trust your advisers and their recommendations enough to follow through with confidence, and they must trust you to provide the accurate and timely information and details they will need to do their jobs right.

Depending on your needs, the cost of these services can range from a very modest few thousand dollars in total to something in the five figures. Even if your resources are very limited, you may still be able to access some professional services, such as those offered by nonprofit firms or other low-cost providers.

Building your Trust Team will take some time and effort, but having people who are on your side will pay off handsomely way down the road. You'll have to make the call about which professional you will need first; if it's March and taxes are due soon, you may need an accountant. If financial needs feel crushing, a financial adviser should be your first call. Or if someone has died, you may need a lawyer to resolve the estate. Top-notch advisers usually can recommend or refer you to other people they trust and who share their commitment to ethics and quality work, making the team building easier as you go along.

Here are the steps to finding the best fit.

FINDING A FINANCIAL ADVISER

Finding the right financial adviser can sometimes seem just as frustrating as trying to find jeans that fit well and flatter. Just about anyone can hang out a shingle and offer financial advice with fairly little training or experience. Insurance salespeople, stockbrokers, accountants, and even lawyers may call themselves financial advisers, though helping you and addressing your specific needs may not be their area of expertise. In addition, even the fanciest credentials may not translate into great work.

What credentials matter? Certified financial planners (CFPs) have completed the equivalent of five college-level classes and passed a ten-hour exam covering a range of financial issues, from budgeting to investing to insurance products in order to earn that designation. Chartered financial analysts (CFAs) have put in hundreds of hours of studying accounting, economics, ethics, math, and finance and passed a series of three six-hour exams. Certified public accountants (CPAs) must hold an undergraduate degree and pass a fourteen-hour exam. These designations also require work experience and additional continuing education each year. Stockbrokers, by contrast, may only have studied for licenses to sell securities.

At the same time, many other designations, such as master financial planner, certified retirement financial adviser, or chartered senior financial planner, mean much less, as they require far less study and simpler or no exams.

In addition to different kinds of training, the varying titles may also come with different obligations to you, the client. Registered investment advisers, CPAs, and lawyers—those who are paid to give investment advice or other advice—have a *fiduciary obligation*, or a legal requirement to put their clients first in making financial decisions. By contrast, stockbrokers and many other so-called financial advisers, whose main job is to follow directions by selling investments or insurance, have only an obligation to recommend options that are *suitable* for you, a far lesser requirement.

"Suitable" investments may be just fine if you're a fairly sophisticated and experienced investor, someone who likes to make your own financial decisions and who understands both stocks and bonds and what it means to hold a diversified portfolio. If, however, financial talk seems like a language beamed down from Mars, you'll want to go with someone who has a fiduciary obligation to put your interests first. (US regulators are considering extending the fiduciary requirement to more advisers, but that hasn't happened as of fall 2011.)

Given the many types of advisers and responsibilities, you would be wise to interview a few different candidates before choosing your adviser. You may find names from friends, people in grief or divorce support groups, or via various professional websites, such as the National Association of Personal Financial Advisors (www.napfa.org), the Certified Financial Planner Board of Standards (www.cfp.net/search/), or the Financial Planning Association (www.fpanet.org).

Here are some of the questions you will want answered:

- *What kinds of services do you provide?* A good financial planner will review your entire financial life, including your current investments, insurance policies, and work benefits. That person should be willing to help you budget, manage debt, plan for both death and taxes, and find the right insurance, as well as help you manage your savings and retirement investments. That person may actually manage your money for you or make recommendations for you to carry out.

- *How do you charge?* Again, you'll find a variety of answers here. Some planners charge by the hour, with fees ranging between $100 and $300 an hour, though they can be higher. Others may charge you an annual flat fee or a monthly retainer for their services. Those who actually take control of and manage your investments typically charge based on your assets under management, with annual charges often running around 1 percent of the value of your holdings. (You'll pay a higher percentage if your account is fairly small or heavily invested in stocks, maybe a lower one if you have an account well over $1 million or own a lot of bonds.) Those advisers may or may not provide other financial services. Still others receive fees and commissions, or only commissions, for selling you various investments or policies, which should raise concerns about whether those are the right products for you. Insurance agents, for instance, may be indispensable for finding you a good life insurance, disability, or health-care policy. But they are typically compensated with commissions. Some products, like whole life insurance and some annuities, may sound great, but often are wickedly complicated, tie up significant cash for long periods of time, have high expenses relative to other options, and pay fat commissions to the salesman. In those cases, before you buy, get a second opinion.

- *Will you be acting as a fiduciary?* In addition to putting your interests first, those with fiduciary obligations also must disclose any conflicts of interest that may affect their decisions and tell you about any fees, commissions, or other factors that could influence the decisions they make on your behalf. If your planner is not a fiduciary, however, then ask specifically what kinds of commissions or fees will be received on any investments or other purchases that are recommended and if there are any conflicts of interest.

- *How often will I hear from you and how often will we meet? Will I work with you personally or an associate?* To some degree, how much hands-on attention you want is up to you. But you do want to work with a planner who will sit down with you at least once a year to thoroughly review your financial situation and check in for updates at least every six months, or quarterly if your situation is complex. A good planner will also call to update you if new legislation affects your situation or when the stock market is in distress, if for nothing else than to calm your nerves.

Sometimes an associate actually can give you much more time and attention than your principal adviser. But you want to be sure that this associate is experienced and qualified and that you can get to your adviser when it's important to you. In addition, your adviser should be aware of and approve any changes to your financial plan.

- *How much continuing education do you complete a year?* Given how frequently laws change, you want an adviser who stays up to date.

- *How much experience do you have?*

- *Have you ever been disciplined by a professional or regulatory body?* Given that a planner might not be quick to disclose problems, you can check out whether an adviser has ever been disciplined through the Securities and Exchange Commission (www.advisorinfo.sec.gov) or the Financial Industry Regulatory Authority (www.finra.org/brokercheck).

- *Can you provide references?* References will give you insight into the planner's professionalism, commitment, and quality. But they aren't foolproof and can be deceiving, so keep your antenna up for any boasts or results that seem suspiciously fantastic. Bernard Madoff, one of the greatest scoundrels of a generation, had the very prestigious post of chair of the NASDAQ board, yet still ran a Ponzi scheme that defrauded innocent investors out of billions of dollars.

- *What is your money management style? How much say will I have in my investments?* There are as many different ways to manage money as there are different investments. Some advisers may put just about everyone into the same investments, while others may tailor selections for every client. Some may buy actual stocks and bonds, others may focus solely on mutual funds or exchange-traded funds (see Chapter 9 for more information on these options), and still others may invest with professional money managers. While any of these could produce good results for you, a good planner will choose the ones that are best suited to your personal situation.

    Even if you consider yourself an investing novice, you need to be comfortable with the amount of risk you are taking, the kinds of goals you are trying to achieve, and exactly what investments are being made. (If you lack confidence in your knowledge, you can also include a trusted family member in your meetings and have copies of all statements sent to that person.) You should be informed about changes to the composition of your portfolio and you should have veto power over anything that doesn't feel right to you. You also should understand what money you'll have access to and how to get it.

Most important, you should feel completely comfortable with your adviser. No matter how great the advice or how talented the planner is, no one else will ever care as much about your finances as you do. If you feel like that person is condescending, speaks in a language you don't understand, or doesn't listen to your concerns, find someone else. This is your money and your financial life and you need to feel confident about how it's being handled, especially during a trying time.

IF YOUR FINANCES ARE TIGHT

Even if you don't have much in the way of savings or investments, a visit or two with a financial adviser who charges by the hour can be useful, especially if you are providing for children. Ideally, for less than $1,000, you can hire someone to review your income and expenses and provide you with the insight you need to get a handle on your situation.

If even that level of service isn't in your bank account—or if you're swimming in debt—a nonprofit credit counselor may be a good option. Usually, the first visit is free and includes a review of your budget and financial situation. If you are eager to get out of debt and the counselor believes you have the means to pay off your debt within five years, the firm will help you put together a financial plan.

Often, that will mean cutting up all but one of your credit cards. You'll pay a modest monthly fee to the credit counseling firm, which will work with your credit card companies and other lenders on a plan to repay your debts over time.

Nonprofit credit counselors are paid, in part, by grants from credit card companies or from a percentage of what is repaid, so they have a strong incentive to help you repay your debts. They can work with companies to reduce late fees, interest charges, and other fees, which can keep your debt from ballooning while you're trying to pay it off. But they don't negotiate to reduce your debt.

There are several ways to find a nonprofit credit counseling firm. Your credit card company must publish an 800 number on each credit card bill that will direct you to a nonprofit firm or provide a few names. You can also go to the National Foundation for Credit Counseling website at www.NFCC.org and put in your zip code. Or, even if you aren't in a bankruptcy situation, you can go to the US Bankruptcy Trustee site (www.justice.gov/ust/eo/bapcpa/ccde/cc_approved .htm) and look up authorized credit counseling firms in your state. Under federal bankruptcy laws, people filing for bankruptcy must agree to some credit counseling and firms that provide that service are vetted by the US Bankruptcy Trustee.

You can also skip a credit counselor and call your lenders yourself to try to work out payment plans. In the aftermath of the financial crisis, many credit card companies and other lenders have been more willing to work with customers who have lost jobs or suffered other setbacks and need a better plan for paying their debts. Sometimes, the companies are even willing to forgive some of the debt. Negotiations can take time and patience, since each situation must be worked out separately. So, if it feels overwhelming or upsetting, you'll probably prefer to let a professional make the calls.

BEWARE DEBT SETTLEMENT AND OTHER PROMISES

If debt is weighing on you, you may be tempted by radio and television ads or telemarketers for debt settlement firms that promise to help get rid of debts altogether. You're better off taking a different course.

While there are some legitimate firms, many debt settlement firms came under fire during the financial crisis for charging large up-front fees, urging customers to stop paying on their debts, and then failing to actually help them. Under new rules issued in 2010, debt settlement firms aren't allowed to collect any fees unless they have provided services, such as settling, reducing, or renegotiating at least one debt, and the customer has made at least one payment to a creditor. In addition, the firms are required to provide a written debt management plan that the customer has agreed to.

Still, be skeptical of any firm that says it can eliminate half or more of your debt or keep creditors from calling you. Some of these firms may be able to get some of your debt erased, but you may be able to do the same thing by calling your creditors yourself. And if you do succeed in settling some of your debt, you should be aware of a significant downside: you may owe income taxes on any debt that is forgiven since the Internal Revenue Service considers that a form of income.

FINDING A LAWYER

You may already have a lawyer who wrote your will, represented you in a divorce or bankruptcy, or someone who provides legal advice for your business. But if you have significant new assets or a newly complicated financial life, you may need a lawyer who specializes in your situation. For example, if you are newly widowed or divorced, you may want to consult an expert in trusts and estates to be certain you have the proper paperwork in place for your family. In this case in particular, a specialist is important because state and federal laws are complex and often changing. Trusts and estates are one area where all your t's should be crossed and your i's dotted (see Chapter 10). Similarly, if you have a serious tax problem, you'll probably want a tax lawyer or a CPA.

Again, you can get referrals from friends or those in similar situations, from your financial adviser, or from your current lawyer. The American Bar Association has a helpful site, www.FindLegalHelp.org, that can direct you to lawyer referral services and other information. Your local bar association may also be able to offer the names of lawyers who specialize in this area.

To check out a lawyer's qualifications and credentials, go to Martindale-Hubbell (www.martindale.com) to see if peers and clients have rated that person's work. To check whether a lawyer has been sanctioned or disciplined, you'll need to check out your state's organization that handles such matters. You can find a list of links to state groups here: public.findlaw.com/library/hiring-lawyer/state-attorney-discipline-links.html.

As with financial advisers, you'll want to know about the lawyer's experience, how you will be charged, what the total cost might be, and whether the lawyer or an associate will handle your matter.

If you need other legal help and can't afford it, contact a local law school to see if there's a low-cost or no-cost clinic available. Many cities also have low-cost legal aid offices that can help you with pressing legal needs.

FINDING A TAX PREPARER OR ACCOUNTANT

Your main need for an accountant likely will be for help with your taxes. (Some financial advisers or lawyers may have enough expertise to take care of your tax filings as well.)

You'll still need to do a fair amount of work, however. Even the most knowledgeable accountant or lawyer cannot fill out your forms without copies of all your W-2 forms, mortgage information, receipts for charitable contributions or business expenses, and myriad other details that go into a tax return. Most providers will give you a checklist of what you must collect so that they can complete the forms.

If your taxes are simple, you can do them yourself using tax-preparation software like TurboTax or TaxCut. For those with incomes under $50,000, the Internal Revenue Service Volunteer Income Tax Assistance program offers free tax help in many cities around the country. (You can get a list by calling 1-800-906-9887.) In addition, the IRS and AARP offer tax help to senior citizens. (For the IRS program, call -800-829-1040. For the AARP program, visit its website, AARP.org, or call 1-888-227-7669.)

If you don't qualify and want help, a chain like H&R Block or Jackson Hewitt is a reasonable alternative. Or another adviser may be able to recommend an accountant.

Ask the preparer if he or she belongs to any professional organization that includes a code of ethics and that requires continuing education. Inquire who will actually be filling out your return and whether that person will be available to represent you in case of an IRS audit. And be sure you understand how you will be billed and approximately how much the service will cost.

A good preparer will ask you lots of questions. The IRS recommends that you stay away from those who guarantee results before they've seen your information or those who promise they can get back a certain percentage of your tax payments as a refund.

No matter who helps you, keep in mind this important point: ultimately, you are responsible for everything on your tax returns. That means you alone must be sure that all the information is accurate and that everything seems proper. If you aren't sure or are confused, it's up to you to quiz the preparer until you are comfortable with the return.

OTHER TRUST TEAM MEMBERS

While the focus here is on professionals who can help you with your financial life, you may find that you also need emotional support. That might come from professional counselors or from various kinds of support groups offered at local churches, community centers, or from other service groups.

You may feel like your situation is unique or that others won't understand what you're going through. No doubt, no one can really know exactly how you feel or how your changed situation has affected you. But chances are someone else has had to grapple with some of the same challenges you are facing and has already figured them out. That kind of experience and perspective is invaluable.

The end of this book has a wide-ranging list of useful websites, including sites that offer more general support to those who are recently divorced, widowed, unemployed, or facing tough financial setbacks.

While your Trust Team can offer important help and support, there are, of course, many adjustments you will have to make yourself. As you build your team, you'll also need to start taking a number of steps toward your new financial life—first and foremost, taking good care of yourself.

CHAPTER 3

TAKING CARE OF YOUR HEALTH

Here's the one big issue that you need to resolve almost before anything else: Do you have health insurance?

If you have adequate coverage through a job or a family member, you can skip this chapter altogether—but don't forget that you still need to take care of yourself during this trying time. Eating right and exercising will be important for your mental health as well as your physical health and will help you better manage the stress of dealing with your new situation.

If you don't have health coverage for yourself and your family, acquiring it needs to be a top priority. Why? Because unanticipated medical bills are one of the very biggest causes of financial disasters, and that's the last thing you need right now.

Even if you're young or incredibly fit and healthy, a car accident or a slide down a slippery staircase could create havoc for you if you aren't insured. Insurance exists to protect you in the event of something unexpected, and health coverage is one of the most important forms. (Purchasing other insurance is covered in Chapter 8.)

The Affordable Care Act passed in 2010 will offer health-insurance choices to all Americans, but many of the key provisions won't kick in until 2014 and many changes to the law could occur between now and then. For the time being, you may have to scramble to be sure you have appropriate coverage that will, at the very least, protect you in an emergency or major illness. Here's how to navigate the maze.

INSURANCE THROUGH EMPLOYERS

If you have lost a job or if you have divorced or lost the spouse who provided your health insurance, you are eligible to continue to stay on the company plan under the Consolidated Omnibus Budget Reconciliation Act, or COBRA. (In the case of a job loss, you and your family may continue your insurance under COBRA for up to eighteen months. If you are divorced or your spouse has passed away, you and your children may continue to be covered for up to three years.) This can be a very expensive option, because the employers can charge you up to 102 percent of the premium for the insurance—which can run more than $1,000 a month. As a result, it may not be the most viable in the long term. But it's one to consider while you look for alternatives.

Despite the steep price tag, COBRA can provide a crucial stopgap while you consider whether you will return to work or shop for your own insurance. Generally, you have sixty days after your life-changing event to notify the employer or the health-plan administrator that you intend to begin COBRA coverage and then another forty-five days to begin paying the premium.

If you have access to coverage at your own work but were covered instead under a spouse's plan, you should be able to start up coverage even in the middle of the year. However, your plan may have a delay before coverage begins, and you may want to sign up for a month or two of COBRA to ensure that you aren't left hanging without any insurance.

Access to health insurance may be one reason to consider taking a job, even a part-time one. Some employers—but not all—offer individual coverage or even family coverage to people who work at least twenty hours a week. It may not be your dream job, or even in your desired field, but in a time of crisis, health insurance may be more important than furthering your career.

INDIVIDUAL INSURANCE

Finding an individual plan is easier than it used to be. Most major insurance companies, including Aetna, Cigna, Well-Point, and UnitedHealthcare, sell plans to individuals. You can apply through their websites or compare rates through an Internet site like eHealthinsurance.com, HealthCompare .com, or your state's insurance division. In addition, a financial planner or financial adviser may be able to recommend a broker who can help you find a plan that works for your budget and needs.

If you feel certain that you will have access to a plan through an employer or a school within six months, or a year at most, short-term health insurance can plug the gap at a much more affordable price than regular insurance. However, coverage is limited, and short-term plans do not cover pre-existing conditions.

If you are under age twenty-six, you can be covered under a parent's plan under the new health-care legislation. A few states, including Florida, New Jersey, Ohio, and Pennsylvania, may allow unmarried children to be on parents' plans beyond age twenty-six.

If you are sixty-five years old or older, you generally are eligible for coverage under Medicare.

If you or your spouse retired from a career in the US military, you may qualify for veterans health care. You may also qualify under other specific circumstances. To find out more, contact your state or county veterans' service office.

If you have a preexisting medical condition and had coverage for at least a year, you'll need to move fairly quickly. If you find a new health insurer within sixty-three days, the insurer must cover your conditions; however, after that period, you may have a waiting period before your preexisting condition is covered. (To prove you were covered, you may need to show a certificate or letter of "creditable coverage" from your insurance company.)

If you are having trouble finding a plan, check to see if any trade groups or religious organizations you belong to offer a group plan. For instance, if you are between the ages of fifty and sixty-four, AARP has arrangements with health insurers in many states to offer both comprehensive and limited health-insurance plans. Those plans may have better terms than what you can buy on your own. Even if you have difficulty finding coverage for yourself, many school districts and colleges offer health-care plans for young people.

Striking out? You may have to consider your state's high-risk pool, which offers insurance to those who can't find insurance elsewhere. Check the website of your state insurance commissioner, which also will have information about searching for private insurance. Again, the coverage may be limited and it may be expensive (though probably cheaper than COBRA), but it's far better than no insurance at all.

As a last resort, the new health-care law also provides for insurance for those with preexisting conditions who have been without insurance for at least six months. You must apply through the government website at www.HealthCare.gov.

CHOOSING A PLAN

Picking health-care plans can be ridiculously complicated. There are many different plan options and ways to pay—premiums (or the monthly cost of insurance), deductibles, co-pays, and money you've socked away in a health savings account or a flexible spending account to help pay bills later. You need to weigh what you can pay for prescription medicines—and decide whether dental care is worth paying extra for.

Unfortunately, there's no way around the fact that health insurance is expensive. Once you accept that, the issue is easier to divide into two main questions: Do you want to pay more for insurance up front, with higher premiums, and then have lower co-pays and deductibles when you get care? Or do you prefer to pay less for your coverage and accept very high deductibles, which means you will pay more when you actually get treatment?

A lot depends on both your health and financial situation. If you have a child with frequent ear infections or you need to see doctors for various issues every year, you may be better off paying more for a comprehensive plan that has lower deductibles and co-pays. That is also true if you have trouble budgeting and would be set back by paying a few thousand dollars in deductibles and other health-care bills.

If you are very healthy and rarely need to see a doctor, and if you have a solid cash account available for emergencies, then you can choose a plan with cheaper monthly payments and much higher deductibles. But beware: some individual plans require that you pay as much as $1,500 to $5,000 in annual deductibles per person before your insurance kicks in, meaning you will mainly have coverage in the event of a serious accident, surgery, or major illness. Sometimes, however, they're the only affordable option available. (On the bright side, if your deductible is large, you can put aside money pretax into a health savings account that can be used to pay medical expenses. See below.)

Pay attention to the titles. *Comprehensive* health plans cover a range of health issues, from colds to catastrophes. By contrast, *catastrophic*, *hospital*, and *preventative* health plans may be much cheaper but they offer limited coverage and will not cover the whole range of potential problems. If you choose those, you take the risk that you'll encounter an issue that isn't covered.

In picking your plan, try to rough out what each option will cost you each year. To do that:

- Add up the annual premiums.

- Multiply the doctor co-pays times the number of doctor visits you expect.

- Compare the deductibles for care and for prescription medicines.

- Multiply the prescription co-pay times the number of prescriptions you think you will need.

- Estimate what you would pay for a mammogram or an MRI, or another procedure you might have during the year.

- Compare the out-of-pocket maximum, the total amount you will pay each year in co-pays and deductibles before insurance picks up everything else.

Add up the preceding amounts. Seeing the total cost may help give you a better idea of which plan best works for you given your financial situation.

OTHER CONSIDERATIONS

Beyond those first decisions about costs, here are other things to consider:

Are you picky about which doctors you see? Most plans have contracts with groups of doctors and hospitals to provide services at a reduced cost. You will pay less if you see these "in-network" providers. Some plans won't pay anything at all if you see a doctor who isn't part of the network; others may require you to foot a much larger part of the bill. If you don't mind sticking to doctors and clinics that are part of an insurance company's roster, you may be able to save a bundle by choosing a plan that requires you to mostly see in-network providers. By contrast, if full freedom of choice is important to you, you may have to pay more for it. (If you have children who attend school out of your hometown, make sure that they can get coverage at their school. Some networks are national, but others apply only to your region.)

Will you need to designate a primary-care physician and will the plan require that doctor's referral to see a specialist? These requirements add another step to the health-care process, but may also lower the cost of your plan.

Do you have costly prescriptions? Some plans offer mail-order services that allow you to get three months of medicine at a time at a much-reduced cost. Deductibles and co-pays on prescriptions can vary, as do the "formularies," the list of medications that are most favored under the plan. If you have a choice of plans and you take medication regularly, it's worth checking to see how each plan treats your particular drugs. (Also, see the information on flexible spending accounts below.)

Should you buy dental coverage if it's offered? Often the cost of the premium is about equal to the cost of two regular checkups a year. But add it up and compare what you would pay your dentist for your cleanings—and then consider whether you are likely to encounter other, more costly issues, like a cracked tooth or broken crown. If you wouldn't go to the dentist unless you had insurance, then you should probably buy it.

Vision care is another piece that typically is optional. Again, you'll need to figure what the annual premium is and compare it with what your needs may be. You may be better off setting aside money in a flexible spending account (see below) to cover contact lenses or new glasses rather than paying for additional coverage.

You don't have much control over what choices any given plan offers. But it helps to understand what will be covered. Look to see how various kinds of medical care will be handled—things like childhood immunizations, flu shots, mammograms, Pap smears, and checkups for children and adults. If you travel a lot or for extended periods, plans usually cover emergency care on the road. But you may also want to know how you'll be covered if you need nonurgent follow-up treatment far from home.

Starting in 2014, even those with preexisting medical conditions are supposed to be able to choose from a range of plans offered by new health-insurance exchanges, but the details of such exchanges and their offerings aren't yet known.

ACCOUNTS THAT EASE THE PAIN

Amid the costs and hassles of health insurance, there are a few bright spots where you can get a break. Some companies allow you to pay your premiums before taxes, essentially getting a discount on the cost. If you are self-employed, you can deduct the cost of buying health insurance.

In addition, you may be able to sock away money into special accounts before taxes to help pay for co-pays, deductibles, prescriptions, and other medical items, including orthodontia and laser eye surgery. Again, using this pretax money is like getting a big discount on the services because you haven't had to pay income taxes or Social Security and Medicare taxes on it.

You or your employer can contribute to a *health savings account* only if you have a high-deductible health plan—that is, one where your annual deductible is at least $1,200 or your family deductible is at least $2,400 in 2011. Under tax rules, the most you can contribute to an account is $3,050 for an individual plan and $6,150 for a family plan in 2011. If you are over fifty-five years old, you can contribute an additional $1,000 to your account.

The account is intended to help you pay for medical expenses until your insurance kicks in. The money can be used for doctor visits, prescription medicines, hospital stays, or most other health-related expenses. What's especially attractive about health savings accounts is that they can be carried over year to year; you do not need to use it up each year. In fact, you can earn interest on the money, which may give you more to cover future health-care costs. And you can take the account with you when you change jobs.

For those who are self-employed or unemployed, or retirees who are too young for Medicare, high-deductible accounts may be the most realistic affordable option. If so, the health savings account can take some of the sting out of having to pay for much of your health care out of your own pocket.

A *flexible spending account* is typically offered through an employer. This allows you to set aside pretax money from each paycheck into an account for health-related expenses. Employers set the minimum and maximum you can contribute, typically a range from a few hundred dollars to as much as $5,000. Under the new health-care law, however, the maximum you can set aside will be limited to $2,500 in 2013.

How does it work? You estimate the amount you will need each fall when your company opens enrollment for its health plan. If you decide to set aside $1,000 a year, your employer will take just under $20 a week from your paycheck before Social Security, Medicare, and income taxes are taken out and keep it in an account that usually is administered by your insurance provider.

The money can be used for a range of items, including deductibles for you and your children, co-pays, prescriptions, orthodontia, laser eye surgery, glasses and contacts, hearing aids, physical therapy, flu shots, and the like. In 2010, over-the-counter products like cold, allergy, and heartburn medicines and pain relievers also could be reimbursed from your flexible spending account, but those rules changed January 1, 2011. Now, to get reimbursed for over-the-counter medicine, you'll need a prescription from your doctor specifying that you need that product. The only exception is for insulin.

Often, the account is linked to your health insurance and when the doctor submits a claim showing that you paid $20 for an office visit or the drugstore submits a prescription that cost you $10 out of pocket, the insurance company will automatically send you that amount from your flexible spending account. Many insurance companies will even directly deposit the reimbursements in your checking account.

You can also submit receipts for expenses directly to the insurance company.

The benefit can be a real help with health care, but it has one hitch: you must use the amount you set aside within a year or a little longer or lose whatever is left over in the account. Many employers give you a grace period of a couple of months, allowing you to spend what's left in your account by mid-March of the following year.

Given the value of the benefit, it's worth spending a little time each fall adding up what you expect to spend out of pocket and figuring out how much to put in the account. Generally, it's better to estimate too low rather than too high. But if you have money left over, it can be a good excuse to update your eyeglasses or stock up on contact lenses.

ADDITIONAL RESOURCES

The government's health-care website, www.HealthCare.gov, has a wealth of information. You can also check your state's insurance commission site, which may have suggestions and search engines for finding insurance and, if you need it, lower-cost resources.

CHAPTER 4

ADAPTING
TO YOUR
NEW REALITY

At this juncture, you may feel like you're just trying to survive. You may feel like you've done plenty if you've begun to assemble your Trust Team and arranged your health insurance. But you also know there is much ahead for you to do.

Admittedly, this is a scary time because you now have to take some concrete steps that will force you to come to terms with your changed situation. You have to get on the phone or online and acknowledge that things are different than they used to be. You have to look carefully at your finances, which may have changed permanently, and decide how you might change the lifestyle you're accustomed to. A root canal procedure probably seems like a whole lot more fun than these tasks.

The silver lining is that these steps probably seem more difficult and intimidating than they really are; in fact, anxiety about tackling them may be worse than actually jumping in. That's because once you address the issues one by one, you should start to feel a strong sense of accomplishment. With each item crossed off the to-do list, with each money issue faced and handled, you are truly taking control of your financial life. And feeling that you're in control and accomplishing what needs to be done should provide very powerful proof that you are doing much more than just surviving—you are moving forward.

UNDERSTANDING YOUR EXPENSES

Even if you may be grieving or struggling to adjust, the bills will still keep coming, the rent or mortgage must still be paid, and you still have to eat. You're forgiven if you've ignored balancing your checkbook or even looking at your bank account since you made that initial assessment of your accounts. But sooner rather than later you have to accept that you cannot spend more money than you have. As a result, you must start assessing whether you have enough income to cover your expenses, and if not, how you will adjust.

In a perfect world, this kind of budgeting or spending plan is complicated because predicting exact expenses is virtually impossible. There are always surprises: the heater goes out, a tire blows, you get sick, or your child gets a wonderful opportunity that comes with a less-than-wonderful price tag.

Your new situation may be even more complex because you aren't likely to have full information just yet about your future finances. You may have gone from two household incomes to one. You may have life insurance coming or a settlement ahead. Or if you've lost a job, you don't know if you'll find a new one quickly or if the search will take months. As a result, you may have to go through this budgeting process more than once in the coming months, so it's okay to make your decisions gradually and to move thoughtfully rather than rushing to slash costs or jump at whatever job becomes available.

To the degree you can, try to maintain some sense of normalcy for you and your family during this transition: you may—wisely—not feel comfortable taking a big vacation right now, but if the kids love piano lessons or soccer, hang on to those at least for a while. If you have lost your job, try to keep your date night with your spouse. If you are suddenly single, make sure your budget allows for some time with friends.

Unless you have no other choice, try to take up to a year to decide whether you need to move. Even if your financial resources have plunged, strive to make changes in steps rather than all at once.

Hopefully, you compiled that list of all your bank accounts, retirement accounts, and other assets, and all your debts, as suggested in Chapter 1. Even if you will be working with a financial adviser, you'll still need to make the time to make some more lists, starting with your absolute necessities and how much they cost. That would include

- Your mortgage or rent payment.

- Utilities, including at least a landline or cell phone.

- Required monthly home maintenance or homeowner fees.

- Groceries and basic toiletries.

- Car insurance.

- Health insurance, co-pays, and prescription medicine.

- Home or renter's insurance.

- Property and other taxes.

- Loan payments, including car loans and credit cards.

- Gasoline or public transportation costs.

- Services that are essential to your well-being or your ability to do your job, like day care or haircuts. If a home security system is essential to your sleeping well at night, it's a necessity. If you never turn it on, then it's not.

It's tempting to just guess how much you spend on each of these, but chances are that you'll be off by a fair amount.

Instead, go for the real numbers by looking at past bills and your checking account for at least three months, since some costs, like doctor visits and insurance payments may vary month to month. Be sure to factor in how your new situation will alter these costs; for example, if there are fewer people in the house, your grocery bill is about to be a lot lower. Or if you've lost the job that required a lengthy daily commute, you may not need to budget as much for gas.

Your checking account may have a feature that allows you to put each debit-card transaction and check into a particular expense category so that you can break down where your money goes. Mint.com, a popular budgeting site, allows you to securely share access to your bank and credit card accounts, if the software is compatible with your bank's system. It will retrieve and sort the information into categories, giving you a quick and clear view of how much you're spending and on what. Like all budget software, it can be a pain to set up—your bank's security software may block it until you change some settings or you may have to manually identify whether an expense is clothing, toiletries, or food. You can also find detailed worksheets at http://online.wsj.com/public/page/booktools .html. If technology isn't your thing, the old-fashioned way of adding expenses up—with pencil and paper—works just fine, too.

Don't worry about the pennies, here. What you're aiming for is a good sense of about how much you must have each month. When you have a rough total of your necessities, add 10 percent to 20 percent to it to account for the things that you don't anticipate that would otherwise ruin your best-laid plans. This is the minimum you need.

Next, tally up your other expenses, the parts of your life that are important but aren't absolute necessities. These include

- Clothes, housewares, new gadgets, or other favorite shopping splurges.

- Dining out.

- Vacations.

- Entertainment, including cable or satellite services or Netflix.

- Gifts.

- Health club.

- Hobbies.

- Home services, such as lawn care, housekeeping, or swimming pool upkeep.

Again, take a close look at how your new situation is going to affect the list. In a perfect world, your necessities would include some savings into a retirement plan, college fund, or general savings, and some charitable contributions, including church or synagogue donations. But depending on your income, they may have to shift to your "above and beyond" list for the moment.

Some expenses, like private school tuition and summer camp, don't fall neatly into a category, but depend on your personal priorities and your family's needs. Classify them based on how important they are to you and your family.

Once you have a broad idea of how much you are now spending and where the money is now going, you need to know if you have enough money to pay for it. First, look at any family income coming in that you can count on arriving at least once a month. That includes paychecks, Social Security payments or pensions, regular investment income, and child support or alimony.

The temptation is to just add it up and consider it your monthly income—but it's not so easy. Before you start spending it in your head, you must take out any Social Security or Medicare and federal and state income taxes that you'll have to pay. Even if you pay taxes quarterly or once a year, you should still reserve for these so that you don't come up short when the time comes.

Now you should have two columns: your new monthly income on one side and your rough monthly expenses on the other. If you've lost a job or lost the provider of a significant income in your household, this may not be a pretty picture. But this isn't your whole picture, so don't despair—this exercise isn't over yet.

If you were recently laid off. If you were dismissed from your job for reasons outside of your control (that is, you didn't quit and you weren't fired for misconduct), you may qualify for unemployment benefits, which are set and administered by each state. Your employer should tell you if you qualify, but you may not know how much to expect to receive until you apply. If you do qualify, sign up for the benefits right away, even if you find it difficult to accept that you've lost your job. In many cases, the process can be completed online, though in some situations, you may have to traipse to a state unemployment office and stand in line. Benefits may take a few weeks to kick in, so the sooner you start the process, the better. In addition, you can't begin designing a new budget until you know what your monthly benefits will be.

Unemployment benefits come with some responsibilities. At the least, you should be available for work and should be actively looking for a new job or taking classes or workshops to prepare you for a job. You may be asked to show proof that you've been searching for suitable employment.

If you take on contract work or a part-time job, that may reduce or eliminate your benefits—but you may still be able to receive your maximum weeks of benefit once the contract work ends. States have different rules, so you'll need to check out yours to know how the rules apply.

Benefits aren't meant to replace a salary, but to help ensure that workers have some funds to live on while they look for new positions. Generally, benefits are less than half what you made before, and they are capped. On average, they run between $300 and $400 a week. Regular benefits are paid for up to twenty-six weeks and may be extended for thirteen weeks or more in times of high unemployment. Since the financial crisis sent unemployment skyrocketing, the federal government has offered benefits for up to a maximum of ninety-nine weeks, though only about half the states offer that maximum. In December 2010, Congress agreed to allow those extended benefits to apply to people who exhaust their regular benefits by December 31, 2011, though it isn't clear what will happen after that.

Keep in mind that all unemployment benefits are fully taxable. While small, they provide some financial boost to help get you through.

If you have lost a spouse. One of the first calls you should make as a widow or widower is to your Social Security office, especially if you have children at home who are younger than eighteen. Dealing with Social Security can seem like working your way through a maze because the rules are complex. But the benefits for children still at home can be substantial and a huge help to the family. In addition to monthly checks, you may qualify for a onetime death benefit of $255.

You can call Social Security, visit a local office, or apply online at ssa.gov/onlineservices/. Before you do, you'll need to collect some papers—though if you can't find them all, don't fret. The staff there may be able to help you.

To prove that you are eligible and to apply for survivor benefits, you'll need the following:

- Proof of death, either from a funeral home or a death certificate

- Your Social Security number and your spouse's

- Your birth certificate

- Your marriage license

A NOTE ABOUT SOCIAL SECURITY SURVIVOR BENEFITS

If you have a child under eighteen who receives Social Security payments after your spouse has died, you will be asked to fill out a form once a year showing how the money was spent.

The Representative Payee form will ask what you spent on food and housing, and separately, what you spent on the total of clothing, education, medical and dental expenses, recreation, and personal items. It will also ask what you saved on behalf of the child.

The child's Social Security payment can be deposited in a family checking account. But if you save Social Security money for the child to use later, it should be put in a savings account dedicated to the child. Beware that when your child reaches the age of eighteen, Social Security may ask that you return any money saved for your child so that it can be paid directly to the youngster when he or she becomes an adult at eighteen.

For that reason, advisers suggest that you spend the child's Social Security funds each year on your child's needs and put away your own money as savings, so that you don't have to worry about returning it later.

- Dependent children's Social Security numbers, if available, and birth certificates

- Your spouse's W-2 forms or federal self-employment tax return for the most recent year

- The name of your bank and your account number so your benefits can be deposited directly into your account

If you are sixty or older, you may be able to collect benefits based on your spouse's total benefit. As a spouse, you may also qualify if you have children younger than sixteen or a disabled child. In addition, children may receive benefits either until they turn eighteen or until they finish high school.

If you and your spouse were already collecting benefits and your spouse died, you will get the higher of the two benefits. If you are divorced, you may be able to collect Social Security based on your ex's work record.

For more information about benefits and applying, go to www.ssa.gov/survivorplan/index.htm on the Social Security website.

If your spouse died while in the US military, you may be eligible for a $100,000 death benefit as well as monthly survivor benefits for you and your children. If your spouse served in the military, particularly during a war, you or your children may be entitled to some veterans' benefits. Contact your state or county veterans' service office, where counselors can help you figure out if you meet the specific qualifications.

If your spouse qualified for a pension or pensions, you will need to contact the employer's benefits department to see whether you are entitled to any pension benefits and when or how you might collect. Look for old 401(k)s or retirement rollover accounts. You may also be able to tap his or her retirement account for living expenses—but check with an investment professional or the company that manages the account first, to be sure you aren't creating a tax problem. In addition, many companies provide life insurance to employees, which may be equal to a year of pay or more. And there may be company stock or stock options that could provide income.

Managing a big sum. As you work through your expenses and your income, you need to figure out how you will allocate any big windfall—a severance package, a divorce settlement, a life insurance payment, or some other kind of inheritance or settlement. For some people, those funds may conjure up images of great cars, second homes, or fabulous vacations. Others may feel so guilty about it that they don't want to touch it. And still others may be frightened by the sheer size and responsibility that comes with having a big pool of funds at their disposal.

In many, many ways, this money may determine the course of your future, so you'll want to take your time and allocate it carefully. Think of it not as a windfall, or found money, but as something more like a safety net—something to keep the bottom from falling out.

Hopefully, you have put the money in a bank money market account or an online savings account. Next, determine whether you'll owe taxes on any of these funds and set aside enough to cover them. If you receive a severance payment for a year's pay at the end of the calendar year, the income may bump you into a higher tax bracket and you may owe more than the company withheld from your check. Life insurance isn't subject to federal income taxes (though it is subject to estate taxes). While property transfers in a divorce settlement aren't taxed, you could face taxes if you sell assets or if you receive some payments as alimony. The last thing you want is to run low on money before you've paid your taxes.

Once you figure out the taxes, you can start to divide up where the money will go. What do you need right away, for immediate expenses? What will you need three months, six months, or two years from now? What do you need long term, such as in your retirement?

Figure out a timeline for what you want the money to cover. For instance, if you've lost your job, you may need some income now; some income later, when unemployment benefits run out; and money to contribute to your retirement account if you end up being self-employed for a time. If your spouse has died, you may want to set aside some money to pay bills now or use a chunk to pay off the mortgage so that you don't have to worry about that monthly payment. Then, some money may go to your retirement, some to the kids' education, and some to supplement your income long term.

Even if the sum is small—say a month or two of severance—try to stretch it out as much as possible. If you aren't going to a workplace every day, you won't need transportation funds, money for eating lunch out, or a new work wardrobe. The longer the money lasts, the better.

Moreover, the more effectively you put each portion of money "away," with an assigned purpose, the less tempted you'll be to splurge, seek "retail therapy," or spend it too quickly or on something that won't last.

FINDING MONEY

By now, you should have a good idea of how much money you'll have each month, what you must spend, and what you'd like to spend. Chances are, you're not where you want to be. Before you get to the really difficult choices—the life-changing decisions like whether to sell a house or put your kids back in public school—you should at least see how much closer you can get to living within your means through smaller, easier steps. In particular, try to come up with ways that will reduce your monthly expenses or that will save you at least $100.

Here are some ways to "find" more money:

- When you do your taxes or when a preparer does them for you, check to see if your withholding is right for your new situation. If you were withholding for a two-income family, you may now be taking out too much for what you will owe. While you don't want to overdo it and face a monster tax bill next year, reducing your withholding to a more accurate amount by filling out a new W-4 form would give you more to live on each month.

- If you have student loans, you may be able to defer your payment for up to three years or switch to a plan that allows you to pay less each month. If you cannot pay your student loans at the moment, you should contact the company that services them right away to try to work out a plan—before you miss a payment, if possible. The government also has several different repayment plans to address different situations, but you need to act *before* you default on your loan. Go to studentaid.ed.gov and click on Repay Your Loans for more information.

- As you look through your budget, what are the costs that you can give up without missing? Are you paying for Netflix, but not using it—or using Netflix, but not watching cable? Are there automatically renewing subscriptions of services that you haven't looked at in ages? If so, cancel anything that you aren't using—that's low-hanging fruit.

- Are you paying your bank monthly fees for an account or overdraft fees for spending more than is in your account? Are you paying late fees on credit cards? Or are you paying for unnecessary "ID-theft protection" or "insurance" to cover credit card bills? Look for a free checking account at a bank or credit union and use free online bill pay as much as possible to cut out the cost of checks and stamps. Set up e-mail or text alerts to tell you when your account is low or when your credit card is due so that you don't incur extra fees for those oversights.

- Take a close look at your cell-phone bill: Are you paying for a lot more minutes than you're using? Are you paying for unlimited texts when a lot fewer would do? Could you give up your Internet and e-mail services on a smart-phone, saving up to $30 a month? Cell-phone services are notorious for creeping expenses, adding a little here and a little there until your bills reach car-payment levels. If you aren't a heavy cell-phone user, you might save a bundle by buying an inexpensive phone and buying the minutes separately, in what is known as a pay-as-you-go plan; careful users can cut their cell-phone costs to as little as $100 or $150 a year, compared with more than $600 for a cell-phone contract.

- Similarly, when was the last time you looked at your telephone bill? The company may have reduced the charge for Internet service—but it may not tell you that until you call and ask. You may be able to combine your landline, Internet service, and cell phone into one package at a lower rate—or give up either the landline or the cell phone altogether.

- Are there services you can cut back, like bringing in housekeeping help every other week instead of every week or reducing the lawn care?

- Are you paying for a storage unit—and do you really need it? If you're storing something you really aren't likely to ever need, toss it and get rid of the storage unit, potentially saving $1,000 a year.

- Hold off on charitable contributions, at least for a few months. Be skeptical of new requests for donations: con artists tend to prey on the bereaved or vulnerable. Plus, you should be sure about your new financial situation before committing funds.

- Depending on how old you are, how old your children are, and how much your assets are worth, you may no longer need life insurance, which is intended to protect your family's income. Along the same lines, you might be able to save a bundle on insurance premiums by raising your deductibles on home and auto insurance. Chapter 8 takes a closer look at insurance and how to review whether you have the right amount.

- If the budget has gotten very tight because your spouse has lost a job or your family income has plunged, it may be better to cut back on savings or retirement contributions temporarily than to have to dig into savings. Ultimately, you're still going to retire, so you'll have to make other changes and resume your savings. But missing a few months probably won't have much of a long-term impact.

- If you are employed, you can also borrow from your 401(k), paying yourself back over time with interest. This has some significant risks: if you lose your job, you will have to repay the loan right away. In addition, the interest you pay may be less than what the money might be earning if it were invested in stocks. Most commonly, this is done to keep up on house payments or for overwhelming medical expenses; it shouldn't be for regular day-to-day expenses. And this, too, should be a temporary move, because this loan will have to be repaid or you'll face tax penalties.

What you really want to avoid, if at all possible, is cashing out your retirement account before retirement age. It's tempting, no doubt, to simply take the money that you invested with a former employer and use it to pay bills—and in some hardship cases, you may be able to tap the funds in your current accounts. But if you withdraw the funds when you are younger, you will pay income taxes on the amount you take out, plus a 10 percent tax penalty. Much worse than taxes, though, is the reality that those funds won't have years and years to grow, and they won't be there for you when you retire.

If you are older than fifty-nine and a half (or you were laid off and you are fifty-five or older), you can start to take withdrawals from your 401(k) and will only owe income taxes on them. But keep in mind that the longer you wait to tap the funds, the longer they will last in your retirement.

HARDER CHOICES

Even if your budget still isn't balancing yet, you may be able to get by on savings for a time. Perhaps your children's school can help with scholarships or your parents or other relatives can assist you with house payments for a few months. If you've exhausted other avenues and your spending continues to far exceed your income, then tougher decisions have to be made. You may need to cut out larger expenses, like country club or health club memberships, eating out, camps, or vacations. You may even need to think about moving from a house to an apartment or liquidating some accounts.

Eventually, you must put all your options on the table. Ultimately, making a financial life work is a balancing act, where you weigh your job possibilities, housing options, school choices, or other costly items against what you can live with and what you can't live without. After all, managing expenses is only half the equation. The other half is managing the income coming in.

Choosing a new kind of work, adding more hours, or taking on a second job are all possibilities, depending on your other responsibilities. Before you start firing off résumés or trying to start your own business, though, figure out how many hours you can realistically work, given your family situation, and how much you need to earn to make ends meet in your current situation. The temptation may be to jump at the first opportunity that comes along, like a low-paying retail job or a great job in another city that requires a long-distance commute. But if the work doesn't offer the necessary pay, or if transportation or child-care costs reduce your take-home pay to well below what you need, then you're going to make matters worse, not better.

In addition to the pay rate, you'll need to figure approximately how much you'll take home. Income taxes, Social Security, and Medicare could take 20 percent to 25 percent off your paychecks right at the start, and then you probably will need to pay for health insurance, parking or public transportation, and, hopefully, a contribution to a retirement account.

If you want to try your own home-based business or work as a contractor, consultant, or freelancer in your old industry, you'll probably need to set aside 30 to 35 percent of your pay for taxes because you'll need to pay both the employee's and the employer's share of Social Security and Medicare, as much as 15.3 percent of pay. (The employee's portion was reduced by 2 percentage points in 2011.) If you haven't worked for a while or if your industry is in the dumps, starting out as a contractor or independent operator in your old business may help you renew and build contacts and refresh or improve skills, allowing you to better compete for jobs that come open.

If your company provides outplacement counseling, try it out; it may prove to be more useful than you think. Also take advantage of social networks like LinkedIn to try to make new contacts.

If the opportunities don't seem good enough, will you need more training to get the kind of job you want? Do you need to go back to school to finish a degree or to learn a new skill? If so, can it be accomplished at an inexpensive community college, or will you need to pay steeper tuition (or maybe borrow) to get what you need?

Of course, work and career questions are rarely easy, especially in tough economic times, and it may take a while to get to the right answer. You can find more guidance, tools, and information at www.wsj.com/careers.

Additional ways to bring your budget into balance and manage your money are addressed in coming chapters, which will dive into credit and credit card issues, housing choices, car and college decisions, insurance, and retirement options.

CHAPTER 5

GETTING
(AND KEEPING)
CREDIT

Credit cards are a necessity of modern life, crucial for booking travel and buying online, handy in an emergency, and a great tool for managing your life day to day if used carefully.

They also come with several special protections that separate them from checks and debit cards. If a merchant doesn't deliver or the product is defective, you can withhold payment and challenge the transaction while you try to work out a solution with the seller. In addition, most card issuers today offer "zero liability," meaning that if your card is lost or stolen, you won't be liable for charges you didn't make.

But what's in your wallet can undergo an overhaul after a traumatic life event, as you reevaluate the kinds of debt you want to have and credit card issuers look at you in a different light.

If you are a disciplined user of credit who pays your bill in full every month, you may benefit from additional perks offered to good customers, like reward cards that can provide cash back, miles for airline tickets, points toward hotel stays, or high credit limits that give you financial flexibility in a pinch. If you typically struggle to stay on top of your bills every month or have grown accustomed to using your credit cards to buy things you can't afford, you may find your options narrowing and your cost of credit soaring now that your financial situation has changed.

Either way, you'll have an easier time rebuilding your financial life if you understand the ins and outs of credit cards and also how creditors see you and monitor you through credit reports and credit scores.

UNDERSTANDING THE CREDIT GAME

Banks and other credit card issuers love for you to have and use their credit cards, one of their most lucrative products—as long as you pay your bills. After all, they earn a little bit of money every time your card is swiped, and some of them charge an annual fee for the privilege of carrying their plastic. Retailers know that people who hold their branded cards, like a Gap or Macy's card, are much more likely to spend more at the stores than people who use generic credit cards.

There's nothing wrong with credit card companies making a profit—but ideally they won't make big profits off you. If you play your cards right, you can use your credit to your advantage, essentially getting free use of money every month and having the flexibility to pay for what you need when you need it. That flexibility could be a particular benefit now, as you cope with a life-changing event.

Many people, however, don't get these benefits because they're not really savvy about how cards work. Here are some common misconceptions.

You only need to pay the minimum each month. Your credit card bill will show the total amount you owe and also a minimum payment, typically about 4 percent of your bill. You must make at least the minimum payment by the due date to stay current on your card.

However, if you only pay the minimum, you'll still pay interest on the whole balance that you owe, at interest rates that are among the highest in the financial world, from a low of maybe 10 percent to as much as 30 percent if you have missed a payment somewhere along the way. Under new rules put in place in 2010, your bill must show how long it will take to pay off your debt if you make only the minimum payment each month—and that's usually a frightening amount of time.

In reality, the minimum payment is something of a ruse, essentially an enticement by credit card companies to get you to pay just enough to keep current while also running up the maximum amount in interest charges. As you accumulate interest charges on each balance, your interest will actually begin to compound not just on what you owe, but also on your interest payments. In other words, you will be paying interest on interest. This is not a good use of your money.

If you cannot pay the entire bill each month, pay as much as you possibly can.

Your credit limit reflects what you can afford. In reality, your credit limit has no relation to what you can afford—or how much you should spend. The credit card company has looked at your record of paying your bills and your previous accounts—not your actual income or net worth—and decided how much it is willing to loan you at one time. It is making an educated guess that you can pay that full amount back—but it doesn't have a clue if you really can because it doesn't know for sure how much income you have right now or how much in savings you might have in the bank.

In a situation where new expenses have just cropped up or your income has suddenly dropped, it may be tempting to look at a credit limit of $10,000, $15,000, or much more as a license to spend that amount. But you will ultimately regret using your entire credit limit. Likely, it will put you in a financial hole. And, as you'll see below, it will hurt your credit score, which is a key way other lenders grade your financial behavior.

The interest rate that I'm charged will stay the same over time. This isn't likely. The Credit Card Act of 2009 put significant restrictions on how credit card companies can raise fixed rates, requiring more notification and preventing companies from retroactively raising your interest rate on your accumulated balance unless you miss payments. In response, most companies that offered fixed rates changed them to variable rates; those variable rates will go up when other interest rates—such as the prime rate used by banks as a reference point for many loans—go up. So the interest rate you paid on balances in 2011 will increase when interest rates go up generally.

In addition, you will pay different interest rates on different kinds of borrowing. If you use your card to get cash—something you should do only in a true emergency—you may pay an annual interest rate of 20 percent or more, which could be twice what you pay for regular purchases.

If you are late making a payment or if your payment on the card bounces, the company can raise your interest rate to its highest rate, often something around 30 percent, and it can keep charging you the higher rate on new transactions well into the future.

The interest rate is the only charge that I'll see. No such chance. Credit card companies will hit you up with all kinds of additional charges when you make a mistake. Did you make a payment after the due date or miss one altogether? You'll be assessed a late fee of as much as $37.

Transferring a balance from one card to another? You'll pay a fee of up to 5 percent of the balance, with a minimum of at least $5. Using your credit card instead of your debit card to get cash? You'll pay another fee of up to 5 percent of the amount, or a minimum of $5 or $10. Using your card overseas? Foreign transaction fees of up to 3 percent of the transaction will be assessed.

In short, the more you rely on the credit card, the more you will pay for the privilege. Using a card that way may make sense in a real pinch—say, when you are out of town and your debit card doesn't work—but it's a terrible habit to get into long term because the interest rates and fees are so high that it can be painfully hard to dig out once you're in the hole. You'll pay more and more just to keep your debt from growing.

On the other hand, if you pay your bill in full every month, the credit card works for you, rather than the other way around.

Special Considerations If You Are Divorcing or Divorced

Credit card companies are all too happy to have two people responsible for a credit card payment, and once you're a joint borrower on a card, you will stay on that card—even if the ownership is with a now-grown child, a parent, or an ex-spouse. There's no law that requires this; it's just that card companies have no reason to let one person off the hook.

As long as you're a joint borrower on any loan, you're responsible for it, even if you are now divorced. To prevent an ex from adding to your debt, you need to separate your credit lives. If you are a joint borrower on a card or cards, you will need to close the accounts, especially if you think there's a possibility that your ex may run up purchases to spite you. Ideally, the balance will be paid off before you close any account. Confirm that the balance is zero before you actually tell the company the account needs to be closed.

If you need to close the account while you still have a balance, you will have some time, perhaps months or even years, to pay off the amount that you still owe.

When you close the account or afterward, you can also apply for a new account in your name only. Depending on your income and your credit record, your credit limit might be more or less than it was originally. It's a good idea to keep at least one account that is only in your name going forward, so you won't have to go through this exercise again.

If you were the sole holder on an account and your spouse was an authorized user, you should be able to cut off his or her authorization with just a phone call.

SPECIAL CONSIDERATIONS
IF YOU ARE WIDOWED

Painful as it is to deal with such details while you're grieving, you need to take steps to protect yourself and your loved one's accounts.

If your spouse had accounts in his or her own name, the credit card company should be notified of his or her death and the account should be closed. That will prevent an identity thief from trying to run up charges on the account and should stop interest payments and other charges from accruing while the estate is settled.

Generally, the estate is responsible for any debts that your spouse owed in his or her own name. However, if you live in a community property state, you may also be responsible for what your spouse owed. (There are nine community property states, in which the income and assets of married couples are assumed to be shared between the two partners: Arizona, California, Idaho, Louisiana, Nevada, New Mexico, Texas, Washington, and Wisconsin.)

If you had joint accounts, you also need to notify the card companies of the death. Some companies will simply remove the spouse from the account; others will issue you a new card on a new account that is only in your name. Because of new rules that require card companies to issue cards only to people who can afford it, you may be asked questions about your income, your assets, and your general ability to pay before a new card is issued. Your interest rate, credit limit, and other terms of the card could change.

If you were an authorized user on a spouse's account, you can ask the card company to transfer the card into your name. However, the card issuer may close the account instead and treat you like a new customer, opening a new account for you based on your current income and assets. (If your spouse was an authorized user on your account, you can cancel that authorization with a phone call.)

As a precaution, you may want to notify the three credit bureaus (see below) of the death to keep crooks from trying to open new credit under your spouse's name. You probably will need to mail in a death certificate as proof. Once that information is in the account, no one should be able to seek new credit under that name. Even if you don't take that step, the credit bureaus update their information from the Social Security Administration regularly, so if Social Security has been notified, the credit record eventually will reflect the death.

GETTING CREDIT

Before you apply for a new credit card or any other kind of loan, you should understand how lenders look at you and how your ability to get credit may be affected by your new situation.

After the huge boom in credit in the mid-2000s that contributed to the financial crisis, the government cracked down on making loans to people who couldn't show they have the ability to pay. Now, a basic requirement for any credit card or loan is that you disclose your income or your assets or both, as a way of showing that you have the money to pay your bills each month. That's only common sense, of course: you shouldn't borrow money that you can't pay back.

Your income doesn't have to be from a job. It could include alimony, Social Security, or pension payments, or money from your savings.

In addition to your income or assets, a lender will look at your credit record and your credit score as a way of estimating whether you are likely to repay your debt. (Lenders aren't the only ones that use credit reports, by the way. Insurers look at them to see if you are likely to file a claim. Employers may check your credit report, especially if you are likely to be dealing with money in your job. Others, such as cell-phone companies and utilities may take a look as well.)

There are three main credit bureaus that maintain a credit report on most Americans:

Equifax, www.equifax.com

Experian, www.experian.com

TransUnion, www.transunion.com

Because some lenders may not report information to all three bureaus, the information in your three credit reports may vary. But generally, you'll find personal information, like your full name and address, your Social Security number, a list of all your mortgages, credit card accounts, education loans, car loans, and other debt, and data about your specific accounts and how you've managed them.

For instance, a credit report will

- note whether credit card and loan payments were made on time, and if not, whether they were thirty, sixty, or ninety days late on any account in your name;

- show the size of your credit limit (or original balance) on each account and also how much you owed on your most recent bill and how long you've had the account;

- reflect if you've filed for bankruptcy, gone through foreclosure, had a financial judgment against you or a lien, or had your wages withheld for failing to pay something; and

- list who has looked at your credit. If you apply for a mortgage, car loan, or credit card, those lenders will look at your report and score, in what is known as a "hard" inquiry. If you are looking for a mortgage rate or a great deal on a car loan and you do your comparison shopping within about thirty days, then all the inquiries on your account will count only as one. Having several different kinds of "hard" inquiries can imply that you're in need of credit and make you look risky. "Soft" inquiries, by contrast, won't hurt you. These occur when you check your own score, when your current credit card companies check your report to see if anything has changed, or when card issuers check your report to see if they want to send you credit card offers in the mail.

Good news will stay on your credit report indefinitely. Bad news will linger like an awful smell, but it will eventually disappear. Late payments and foreclosures will remain on your record for seven years, while bankruptcies can appear for up to ten years. A short sale, where you sell your house for less than the mortgage, may also appear on your credit record for up to seven years if the lender chooses to report it to the credit bureau.

For all that information, an awful lot of important facts about you are not in your credit report. An employer may be listed, but the credit bureaus don't use that information or keep it up to date. The bureau doesn't know your income or how much you have in savings or in your retirement account. A number of details that may make you creditworthy may be on a credit application, but not in your credit report.

Given that you've had a major change in your life, you should keep a close eye on your credit report to be sure that information is accurate and that no one has tried to steal your identity. You can check each of your three credit reports for free once a year. That means you can look at them all at once or spread them out and look at one bureau report every four months. If you worry about identity theft, it's best to look at them one at a time, so you will know more quickly if something suspicious appears. Access your reports at www .annualcreditreport.com, following the instructions and ignoring all the sales pitches for credit monitoring or scores, most of which aren't worth the cost.

If you see a mistake, use the online dispute tools to challenge it, call the phone number on your credit report, or write a letter to the address listed. The accuracy of your credit record is crucial for making sure that your credit score is the best it can be and that you are giving the right impression to potential lenders, insurers, and even employers that may check your credit report.

KNOWING THE SCORE

Using the information in your credit report, the bureaus also calculate a credit score for you. The most widely used score is the FICO score developed by Fair Isaac Corporation. Because each bureau may have slightly different information about you and may use different versions of the FICO score, your score may vary from bureau to bureau.

The FICO score is a number between 300 and 850 that seeks to predict how likely you are to pay your bills. Generally, a score above 740 is considered excellent and will qualify you for the best interest rates and terms. Until the financial crisis, people with scores of 580 or higher were usually able to get a mortgage or other loan. But in 2011, your minimum score may need to be above 600 to qualify for a loan, and often above 700 to get decent interest rates and to qualify for mortgage insurance, which is required if your down payment is less than 20 percent. Those cutoffs will vary by lender and how the economy is doing.

What's most striking about the credit score process is how quickly you may be penalized for making one mistake. If you're going through a financial crisis, lost your job, or your spouse has died recently, paying all of your bills may seem like a low priority. But missing payments could cost you in financial flexibility.

The most important factor in your FICO score, accounting for 35 percent, is whether you pay your bills on time. Being thirty days late on one mortgage payment can knock up to 100 points off a score—reducing a pristine score of 780 to the high 600s, which is the edge of subprime territory. A score that starts at 720 or 680 will fall by fewer points, but will more quickly reach a level where new credit is very hard to acquire.

Assuming that's your only mistake, returning to your original score can take up to three years—even if the late payment was made by an ex on a joint account.

If you continue to miss mortgage payments and the house goes into foreclosure, your score may fall by as much as 150 points from its peak, dropping your score to the high 500s or low 600s, a point where getting loans at reasonable interest rates is nearly impossible. In that case, returning to your original score may take seven years—the length of time the information stays on your credit report.

A number of missed payments or defaults will have a deeper impact. The more recent the missed payment, the more it will affect your score. If you missed the payment by mistake, you should call the lender right away and explain. If you have been a good customer, it's possible that the lender will forego reporting your error to the credit bureau.

(Typically, lenders don't report a payment as late until thirty days have passed and you're in danger of missing a second payment. If you simply pay a credit card bill after the due date but before it is thirty days late, you probably will be charged a late fee but that probably won't show up on your credit report.)

The second most important factor, affecting 30 percent of your score, is how much you owe, particularly how much of your available credit you've used. The bureau will list your balance on each credit card as the amount you owed on your most recent monthly bill. It doesn't use a real-time balance, like the one you see when you look at your accounts online. It also doesn't know how much you pay each month. So even if you pay your bill in full every month—the smart thing to do—the credit bureau doesn't know that and it isn't a part of your credit score.

The score will weigh how much is owed on each account against your credit limits. It will consider both the percentage of credit used on each account and the percentage of your total credit that you've used. To get the best scores, you should use less than half of your available credit, and ideally, less than 30 percent. That is, if you have a $10,000 credit limit on your card, try to keep your borrowing to $5,000 or less, and preferably below $3,000.

If you have accumulated big charges on your credit card while you were in the midst of a crisis, you should know that the impact of this is less severe than missing payments. Once you pay down or pay off your debt, your credit score will adjust fairly quickly to reflect your lower debt levels.

The remaining 35 percent of your score is based on three other factors: the types of accounts you have, how long you've had your accounts, and the number of credit inquiries or recently opened accounts. The longer you've had your accounts, the more you show that you can handle credit responsibly. This factor penalizes young people, who simply can't have had accounts for very long, but it rewards people who stay with the same credit card or pay off a mortgage over a long period of time.

Closing an account can penalize you because it reduces the amount of credit available to you and it changes your credit history. Sometimes you have to close accounts because of divorce or the death of a spouse. But if you no longer want an account and don't have to close it, simply cut up the card. The lender will eventually close the account because of inactivity. Closed accounts may show up on your credit report for several years, meaning you still get some credit for them.

The score doesn't consider whether new credit is good (like refinancing a mortgage to a lower rate) or bad (like applying for credit you don't need). Rather, it just looks at how many lenders have pulled your record with "hard" inquiries and how much new credit you've lined up. The more new credit you have, the more likely it will hurt your score. Inquiries stay on your record for two years, but often only affect your score for a year or so.

The scoring formula also looks for a mix of accounts, like a mortgage, car loan, education debt, and credit cards. Certain types of debt, like loans from finance companies, may be considered more risky because they are considered lenders to those who are less creditworthy. That's one reason why you should be choosy about opening debt accounts and only sign up for cards or credit that you really need.

Because information about your savings or retirement accounts, your income, employment history, and other factors aren't in your credit report, they aren't reflected in your credit score, either. Nor is your age, marital status, race, or gender part of the score.

If you want to see your credit score, you can buy your TransUnion and Equifax FICO scores from MyFico.com for $20 each. Experian doesn't sell a FICO score.

If all of this isn't confusing enough, it gets more so: all three of the credit bureaus sell or provide other scores—including the Vantage score that they developed together, as well as their own scores. These scores may reflect your creditworthiness, but they use different formulas and maybe even a different range of scores. In addition, a number of websites, like CreditKarma .com, offer free credit scores—but they aren't FICO scores. Those sites are useful for understanding what goes into a score, but they're like buying generic soda instead of Coke; they aren't the real thing.

Under a new law that took effect in mid-2011, if your credit score is the reason you are denied credit or you didn't receive the best terms, the lender must provide you with a free copy of the credit score that was used. Ideally, though, you'll have a sense of your score before you apply for credit so that you have some sense of what options are available to you.

HOW TO CHOOSE A CREDIT CARD

If you're starting over with credit or if you have to open your own accounts, you first need to be brutally honest with yourself about how you're going to use the card.

Are you going to carry a balance? If so, you need to shop

for the lowest interest rate you can get. Some cards offer teaser rates, or lower rates for a limited time, but that won't really help your finances if you're still paying interest charges when the introductory period ends. Instead, shop around for the card with the best post-teaser rate that fits your credit rating.

If you pay your bill in full every month, then a low interest rate doesn't really mean much to you. Instead, look for the most lucrative rewards in the form of travel miles and perks or cash back. You should decide up front if you think it's worth paying an annual fee of $50, $75, or $200 for rewards privileges or if you want to look for cards that offer some rewards and no annual fee. If you travel a lot, a rewards card that offers miles or points that can be used for airfare or hotels can be a real perk. If you don't travel much, however, stick with a cash-back card that will reward you with green stuff that you can use anywhere.

In most cases, you're going to be better off with a Master-Card, Visa, Discover, or American Express card than with a card from a major retailer or gas station. Even if stores tempt you with great discounts for opening an account, those offers are plentiful and not very useful. You only need a couple of credit cards in your wallet—one for regular use, and one for emergencies or when your main card doesn't work—so you don't need to fill all the slots with other cards.

It's simplest to begin your search where you bank and do other financial business. After all, you're already a customer. And it is easier to manage your money online if all the accounts are in the same place. But if your bank's offers are lacking or you just want a better deal, then you can search for low-rate cards at a number of websites, like NerdWallet.com, CreditCards.com, Credit.com, LowCards.com, and CardHub .com. All those sites get payments from some card companies for referring customers, so take the recommendations with a grain of salt.

IF YOU ARE REFUSED CREDIT

If you have never had credit in your name or had very little, you may have trouble getting it because you have what's known as a "thin credit file." Similarly, if you have poor credit because of a bankruptcy or foreclosure, you may find it difficult to reestablish yourself. The following are some options, however, that will help you establish a credit record or land a credit card.

- Try applying for a retail or gas card. While these aren't the best cards to have—they often come with very high interest rates—they can be easier to open than other cards, often because they have fairly low credit limits. If you're starting out, or your credit is banged up, landing and managing a retail or gas card or two for a year or so can help bring your credit score up to a decent level.

- Apply for a secured credit card. A secured card is backed by your own money so that the credit card issuer is taking very little risk. For instance, you might deposit $500 in an account. The bank would issue a secured card with a $500 credit limit. If you fail to pay, the bank can tap your account. Secured cards often come with additional fees and aren't ideal. Lenders may not report your payment record to the credit bureaus. But after a year or so of on-time payments, you often can convert a secured card to an unsecured, or regular, credit card.

- Become an authorized user on someone else's card. If you're serious about paying your bills and doing it on time, ask a family member, like a parent or sibling with good credit, if he or she will make you an authorized user on an account. Then make good on your promise and repay the cardholder promptly when you use the card. In addition to having access to a regular credit card, you will benefit from the good credit record your family member has built up. Just be sure to use the card responsibly; if you run up a bunch of charges, the holder is responsible for them. Don't forget that you can be cut off with a phone call, leaving you back where you started.

HOW TO IMPROVE YOUR CREDIT SCORE

If your score has suffered from a rough patch, it will take time and diligence to bring it back to a level where you qualify for good credit. But scores change all the time and improvements can happen, in some cases rising by one hundred to two hundred points over a year or two.

A lot depends on what kind of trouble you've had. If you are simply maxed out on your credit cards, but you're continuing to pay the minimum amount on time each month, you can send your score climbing just by paying down your debt. That's hard work, but it can pay off in more financial flexibility and the relief from knowing that you aren't underwater anymore.

If you are juggling several cards with large balances that are dragging you down, you may feel like you can never pay them off. The ideal strategy is to make a list of all your debts and the interest rates you are paying. Make the minimum payment on each card except the one with the highest interest rate. Pay as much as you can on that card every month until it is paid off, and then start paying off the next highest card. Put any tax refund or any additional money you have each month toward reducing that balance. As each card is paid off, you'll have more money to put toward reducing your other debts.

If that seems too complicated, then take the simpler route: Pay off the smallest balance first and then the next smallest. It may not be the most financially efficient, but you'll have a great deal of satisfaction in eliminating a debt and seeing your progress. By the time you get to your biggest debt, you should have more money available to put toward paying it off. Avoid balance transfers, which usually involve opening a new account and additional fees when you transfer money. Though the teaser rate or the promise of no interest for six months may look promising, you could still end up paying interest. You are much better off working to reduce the debts you have.

If you have missed several payments, it may take a year or two of consistently paying on time to bring your score back up. Though missed payments stay on your record a long time, they become less of a factor after about two years.

Foreclosures and short sales, and other situations where creditors had to write off debt loaned to you, linger longer. But if you trim your debt and pay on time, you may be able to bring your score back to a level where you can get new credit—albeit at a higher interest rate—in two to three years, especially if you have a long credit history with few other blemishes.

Bankruptcies, however, are the toughest to recover from. Experts say that you'll need at least three years of good credit behavior to restore your credit to a reasonable level after a bankruptcy proceeding. It could take longer, depending on how much debt you had and whether you have enough credit left to rebuild your track record by showing that you can stay on top of your bills. That said, you may be able to get a credit card, likely at a very high interest rate with a small credit line, because you won't be able to discharge it through bankruptcy again for a number of years.

As noted in Chapter 2, avoid people who say they can fix your credit or make debt disappear. Many of them overstate their ability to help you, and in many cases, your credit report may be worse off if debt is discharged than if it's paid off. You may end up with a big-time tax bill as well.

Instead, you need to look at your new situation and figure out the best strategy for paying your bills on time and whittling down your debt. Once you're back on track, many more opportunities will become available to you.

PROTECTING YOUR IDENTITY

Identity thieves can strike anyone, but they particularly prey on the vulnerable and distracted, such as those who have just lost a loved one or suffered another kind of setback.

Often, the thievery becomes apparent when an unauthorized charge appears on your credit card or bank account statement. But when someone opens credit in your name, using your personal information, and has the bill sent to an address other than yours, the crime can go undetected for months. (While the perpetrators may be strangers who bought your information on the Internet, they also could be roommates, friends, relatives, or coworkers.)

That's a huge reason why you should check your credit reports at least once a year, or check one of your three credit reports every four months. Ignore the irrelevant information, like whether your middle initial is correct, and focus on whether all the accounts listed belong to you. If they don't, notify both the credit bureau and the security or fraud department of the creditor immediately.

More details about what to do if you suspect identity theft can be found at the Federal Trade Commission website, www.ftc.gov.

The following are other steps you can take to prevent identity theft:

- Guard your personal identification number (PIN) carefully and don't share it beyond your most trusted family members. In addition, cover your hand when you type it in at the ATM or the store, to prevent an onlooker or hidden camera from recording it.

- Be sure that any e-mail or letter you receive saying that your address has been changed is accurate. If you haven't received a bill in a while, call the lender to check on it.

- Be aware that phishing e-mails can look an awful lot like real bank, brokerage firm, and retailer e-mails. If you want to follow up, use your browser to go to the website rather than clicking on a link from the e-mail. Never give out your PIN, password, or credit card number in response to an unsolicited e-mail or phone call.

- Don't save your ID or password on a public computer or any computer that can be accessed outside your family.

CHAPTER 6

DECIDING WHETHER TO STAY OR MOVE

This may be the most wrenching decision you have to face after a financial setback: Do you stay in your house or do you move?

Some people mistakenly see homes purely as investments, or as veritable piggy banks. But your home, the center of your family life, is much more than just a financial arrangement, especially after a personal loss or trauma. Your home can be a shelter from the personal storm, the one place where you can let your hair down and put your feet up. It's the place you have arranged just so, with all your favorite things around you. And if your children are still living there or coming home frequently, it can provide emotional stability for them at a time when they may be feeling insecure or anxious.

But for all the sentiments and memories tied up in a house, there's also a bottom line: you have to be able to pay the mortgage on time, pay the taxes and insurance, and keep it maintained, regardless of where home prices or mortgage rates are at the moment. In many cases, savings, life insurance, the equity you've built in your house over the years, and your careful financial management can make that a realistic proposition. But if your household income has dropped substantially and you don't have much of a cushion, keeping the house could be such an overwhelming challenge that it simply isn't worth the struggle to try to stay.

The recent housing debacle may complicate your situation. Home prices in some areas have dropped by 40 percent or more since the 2006 peak (and in many cases, show no signs of bouncing back), meaning the equity (or your ownership stake) that you may have counted on is no longer there. In addition, if you took a second loan out on your house or if you have tapped an outstanding home equity line of credit, that additional debt may limit your options by making it harder to refinance or negotiate a lower payment.

Still, plenty of options are available, depending on your finances, your current home value, your mortgage, and how important your home is to you. Before you can make this life-altering decision, you will need to do some math and weigh the possibilities.

WHAT CAN YOU AFFORD?

Asking how much you can afford to spend on your home is something of a trick question. In some parts of the country, like New York City, you have almost no choice but to spend a ridiculous percentage of your pay on housing. And you can spend a lot in other places if you really want to.

But in most parts of the country, a general rule of thumb is that you shouldn't spend more on housing than 28 percent to 33 percent of your total income—all your pay, child support, investment income, and any other money coming in, added together before taxes. And that cost would include your property taxes and your home insurance.

But that's a maximum, not unlike that credit card limit in Chapter 5. If you have children at home, large medical or education expenses, or other debt, spending 33 percent of your gross income won't give you much wiggle room in a budget that also has to cover utilities, food, health insurance, retirement and other savings, and income and payroll taxes. In many cases, aiming for 28 percent or less of your gross income is a much more comfortable equation.

Lenders use another rule of thumb: your total debt payments shouldn't be more than 36 percent of your total income. Say you make $75,000 a year, or $6,250 a month. Your total debt payments shouldn't exceed $2,250. Again, that would be a stretch on any budget, leaving little for unexpected expenses—or potentially resulting in more debt if you suffered another setback.

Still, to see how that debt equation would play out, consider if you had a $500 a month car payment, $200 a month in education loans, and another $250 a month in credit card payments. You would have $1,300 left for a mortgage payment, plus real estate taxes and insurance. If mortgage rates are around 5 percent, as they were in 2011, and you put down about $10,000, you probably could afford a $175,000 home, which would be a decent house in many parts of the country. But if mortgage rates jump up to 7 percent, your budget will buy you something more like a $140,000 home.

If you have a handle on your budget and your other expenses, you can do your own personal calculations based on your own spending and comfort level. Add up your regular monthly expenses outside of housing, including some money every month for savings. Allow yourself some cushion so that your budget isn't so tight that an unexpected problem rips a hole in it. What's left over? (It's probably less than 28 percent of your gross pay.) Is it enough to cover what you're paying now?

If not, moving may be a good option. But you should also weigh not just your moving costs but additional costs of making a move. Would you save any money renting in a neighborhood that is safe and close to friends, family, and the right schools? Would you have to send your kids to private school? Would your commuting costs change?

Is there cheaper housing in an area that is acceptable for you and your family? If the savings are large and they give your family significantly more financial flexibility, a move may turn out to be a wonderful decision. On the other hand, if you're already living in a modestly priced area, you may not have many cheaper options that will work for you. Or moving may be just too jolting to your family. If so, you'll want to also consider your financial options.

Option 1: Refinancing and Other Borrowing Possibilities

One question to consider is whether refinancing your home or taking out a second loan will help you without putting you in a debt bind. To refinance your loan, you need the following:

- Equity in your home

- A good credit record

- The ability to prove that you can make your payments

If you have those, you may be able to save some money and improve your situation by refinancing. (If you are going through a divorce, you may have to refinance your home just to settle your split.) But whatever you do, you don't want to treat your home like a bank account. Though soaring home prices in the mid-2000s left some people believing that houses were wonderful, reliable investments, that assumption turned out to be built on a foundation of sand. Over time, home prices have consistently climbed at about the same rate as inflation; that is, they keep up with general price increases but don't usually exceed it. Sometimes, prices do go up fast. But sometimes, they also plunge in a matter of months and stay down for many years.

If you want your home to be both a nest and a nest egg for you, you need to manage the financing and your equity with care, limiting your risk and drawing on your equity only in very limited situations.

That said, reworking your loan could be the ticket you need to help you keep your home. To figure it out, start by doing some math, comparing your mortgage rate to the current rates being offered. But don't apply for loans just yet; you'll be better off waiting until you know exactly what you're looking for. Because lenders must check your credit score when you apply to see what rate you qualify for, you want to do all your loan shopping in about a thirty-day period.

You can look up mortgage rates in your area on BankRate .com or HSH.com or check listings in your local newspaper. A real estate agent can also put you in touch with reliable mortgage brokers and lenders.

You can estimate your payments by using the mortgage calculators on those websites. As an example, say you are paying 6.5 percent on a 30-year mortgage that started at $200,000, resulting in a payment of about $1,264 a month. If rates for 30-year fixed mortgages are around 5 percent, as they were in 2011, your payment could drop to about $1,074 a month, saving you $190 a month or more than $2,000 a year. If you have paid off some of your mortgage and need to refinance only $150,000 instead of $200,000, your new payment could drop to as low as $805 a month. That would save you $459 a month, or more than $5,000 a year.

You also can save big if you currently are paying on a 15-year loan and can refinance to a 30-year loan. For instance, say you are paying on a $200,000, 15-year fixed-rate loan at 5 percent. Your monthly payment would be about $1,582 a month. If you refinanced to a 30-year loan at 5 percent, your payment would fall to $1,074, a savings of more than $500 a month.

But that isn't the whole equation. Refinancing can be difficult and expensive. You'll need to show that you have the assets and income to pay for the loan, providing pay stubs, tax returns, bank statements, and other documentation. To get the best rate at the time this was written, you would need a credit score of 740 or higher. An appraiser must determine that your house is worth more than the loan amount. If the value of your equity—or the amount of the house that you own outright—has fallen to less than 20 percent, you'll have to pay for private mortgage insurance as well, which adds a little more than half a percentage point to the interest rate you'll pay, reducing your savings.

Once you know what kind of loan you want, you'll want to shop around, calling at least three or four different lenders. You want to know their best rate for the loan you want, whether you'll pay any origination fees or discount points (fees that mortgage providers charge), and what the estimated closing costs would be. Title insurance, which is regulated by states, should be the same at all the lenders in your area, but other closing costs can vary widely.

Total closing costs may run from 3 percent to 5 percent of the value of the loan, or roughly $8,000 on a $200,000 mortgage. Those costs can be rolled into the loan—but that will raise your payment slightly and you will pay a lot of interest on that money over time. At the least, you'll want to stay in your house long enough to earn back what you spent to get the loan. So if your savings were $200 a month, or $2,400 a year, you would need to be in your house more than three years to earn back $8,000 in closing costs.

With a new loan and a lower payment, you'll still be able to deduct your mortgage interest on your tax return, but you may be paying less interest, and thus, have less of a deduction. However, if your family income has dropped and you're in a lower tax bracket, that drop in tax savings won't be nearly as big as your monthly savings.

Then there's another factor: you'll be starting the loan clock again at thirty years, meaning you will pay an awful lot of extra interest if you stay in the house for three more decades. But if your goal is to keep the house for a limited time and you'll be moving on in seven or ten years, the monthly savings could be a big help to your budget.

Keeping those risks in mind, here are a few other considerations and ways to refinance:

- If possible and if the rates are reasonable, like 7 percent or
  below, opt for a fixed-rate mortgage. There is great reassur-
  ance in knowing that your rate won't leap up on you as interest rates climb. In addition, if your income goes up with
  inflation or pay raises, your mortgage will stay the same, giving you more cushion in your budget.

- If you don't plan to stay in your home more than five or
  seven years and the interest payments on an adjustable
  rate mortgage, or ARM, are much lower than fixed-rate
  loans, you might want to consider that route. Some ARMs
  have rates that stay fixed for one year, three years, five
  years, or longer before they start moving along with a specific index. Others adjust every year. The initial rate nearly
  always is very attractive—but you can't focus on that. Instead, you need to understand how much your rate might
  go up at any one time and how high it could ultimately
  climb. If you aren't going to be in your home very long,
  then you may never hit that highest rate, and the low rates
  of the first few years may be worth it. But you shouldn't
  sign on unless you could make the highest payment if you
  had to.

- If you have a lot of equity in your house, you may be able to
  do a "cash-out refinance," in which you take some cash out of
  your home while refinancing your mortgage. For instance, a
  couple with a home valued at $400,000, with $100,000 left on
  the mortgage, could refinance to a new $200,000 loan, tak-
  ing about $100,000 out of their home equity. Typically, the
  cash is used to renovate or maintain the home, or sometimes
  for education expenses. If you use this money for daily living
  expenses, it probably won't last very long, and you could find
  yourself with a big house payment and little flexibility. If you
  get in over your head, you could lose your house.

- If your home has fallen so much in value that you don't have enough equity to refinance, you may qualify for the government Home Affordable Refinance Program, which allows you to refinance a loan that is up to 125 percent of your home's value at current market rates. That is, if your mortgage is $250,000 and your home is only worth about $200,000, you still may be able to reduce your interest rate and your payments under the program, which has been extended to June 30, 2012. To qualify, you must be current on your payments and your loan must be owned or guaranteed by Fannie Mae or Freddie Mac, the two big government mortgage players. To learn more, go to MakingHomeAffordable.gov.

- If you are at least sixty-two years old and own your home outright, you could consider a *reverse mortgage*, which allows you to receive a lump sum or a stream of monthly payments that come to you. You continue to own the home and pay taxes and insurance. But if you move or die, proceeds from your home sale will go to repay the loan. Such loans come with fairly high fees and are complex, but they offer people who own their homes a chance to tap their equity for living expenses without having to move. A reverse mortgage counselor certified by the Department of Housing and Urban Development can walk you through the process and help you decide if it makes sense for you.

- One other financing option is a "home equity line of credit," sometimes called a HELOC (pronounced hee-lock). The line of credit is a second loan on your house, with a variable interest rate, that you can draw on up to a maximum amount, sort of like a credit card. The interest rate may start out low, but it can climb quickly if interest rates rise in the broader economy. You pay the interest monthly and can repay the loan over many years. Some banks even issue debit cards tied to the loan. Because this loan is backed by your home, it should be used cautiously for home repairs or improvements, education, or to pay overwhelming medical bills. You'll need good credit and equity in your home and there will be some up-front costs. Have a clear plan for how you will repay it, just as you would repay credit card debt. Ideally, a HELOC would be used only for a temporary need, such as fixing up a home to sell it, rather than used as an open-ended loan, since it puts your home ownership at risk.

- Banks also offer second mortgages at fixed rates. In the old days, people took out a second mortgage to remodel the kitchen or add a wing. But in recent years, the rates on second loans have been so unattractive that it usually is much cheaper just to refinance your loan.

OPTION 2: PAYING OFF THE MORTGAGE

If you received a life insurance payment or a large cash settlement as severance or from a divorce, you may be tempted to pay off your mortgage to cut your housing expenses dramatically. Your housing costs won't go to zero, of course—there will still be property taxes, home insurance, and the usual maintenance and upkeep—but getting rid of the mortgage will save you boatloads of interest over the life of a loan and will be less of a hassle than taking out some money every month to help with the mortgage payment. It can also take a huge burden off the family budget and might help you sleep better at night.

That doesn't mean it's always the right thing to do, however.

Financial experts also note that when you pay off your mortgage all at once, you may be limiting your future returns. If your mortgage is at 5 percent, that's what you'll essentially earn by paying it off. But you might be able to earn more by investing the money in a mix of stocks and bonds. That's a consideration, but it may not outweigh the peace of mind of knowing that you can stay where you are even on a permanently reduced income.

The bigger question is whether you'll be locking up too

much of your cash and your net worth in an asset that is il-liquid, or hard to sell, making you asset-rich and cash-poor. You may own your house outright, but you may not be left with much cash at your disposal, which could be a challenge if you want to take a great family vacation, send a child to col-lege, or pay for a significant medical treatment. In a real cri-sis, you could have to sell the house or end up with a new mortgage.

As with any financial equation, you need balance. You want to have access to a certain amount of cash in case of an emergency, access to other liquid assets such as mutual funds or stocks and bonds for longer-term or bigger ticket issues, and also hold some funds that are essentially untouchable un-til you retire. So if you want to pay off a mortgage, the ques-tion you need to resolve is how much cash you'll be spending and how much you'll have tied up in the house relative to what's still accessible to you. If you have $1 million in life in-surance and only $75,000 left on the mortgage, then you're probably making a comfortable decision. But if paying off the mortgage means that all your savings will be tied up in real es-tate and retirement funds, don't do it. You'll be better off pay-ing yourself a bit each month from your cash funds to cover the mortgage than tying up all your money.

If at least half of your liquid assets are still available to you and that seems like a reasonable amount of money to fund what you'll need to pay for in the next five to ten years, then it may well make good sense. As with any of these decisions, a fi-nancial planner can help you sort through the issues and come to a conclusion that works best for you.

OPTION 3: CREATIVE FINANCING

How determined are you? If you truly want to stay in your house and the cash flow isn't cutting it, consider whether these creative options might work for you:

Can you rent a basement, upstairs, or a room to a student

or young person who needs a reasonable rent and doesn't have many other space needs?

If you're paying for in-home child care, would you save money by having a live-in nanny or au pair, who would require less cash pay in exchange for a place to live?

Is there a relative who would be willing to loan you money for your home, giving you access to extra cash for the mortgage or even buy the house outright and rent it back to you? In the former, that relative would be privately refinancing your debt and would have to be paid back first when you sell the house. You should get any agreements in writing, so that there aren't misunderstandings later. But sometimes those with more financial wherewithal are willing to help out.

PROPERTY TAXES AND OTHER HOME EXPENSES

Unlike your monthly mortgage payment, property taxes are due less often. In many cases, taxes and home insurance are wrapped into your mortgage payment and the mortgage company will collect them every month and then pay them once a year. But if you pay off your mortgage, you'll want to set up a new system for putting funds away so that you aren't surprised by a big tax or insurance bill. It may make sense to set up a new savings account for that money so that it's out of your checking account and also earning a little interest.

MOVING ON

After careful consideration, you may decide that it's best for you to sell your home and relocate, perhaps to save money, find more employment opportunities, or be closer to those you love. Unless you're a very good negotiator with a great understanding of real estate and your current market, you'll probably fare best if you hire a real estate agent to help you.

As with choosing any professional, you'll want to interview

at least two or three different people. You'll want to learn about their sales styles, how they would market your house, what price they would recommend that you start at, and what suggestions they have to make your place more attractive to potential buyers before choosing one of them. In a slow and demanding buyers' market like the one that has persisted since the financial crisis, a fair bit of luck will be involved as well. But you will want the best advice you can get from someone who knows your neighborhood and understands what kinds of people are looking.

Almost everything related to selling a house is potentially negotiable. Generally, real estate agents represent the seller, though some agents represent the buyer only. The seller usually pays the full commission, often 6 percent, though that may vary in your region. But commissions may also be negotiable, depending on the price of your home and other factors. You should consider what you might accept as a price, how much you might be willing to fix to land a buyer, whether you might help with the buyer's closing costs, and whether you need to offer any special incentives, like an allowance for painting or carpeting the house. You'll also need to be ready to make your own move quickly, in case a buyer shows up who wants to take possession right away.

A good agent will bring you information about sales of comparable homes in your neighborhood and help assess whether your house should sell for more or less. To some degree, there is guesswork involved; no one knows exactly what a buyer will want, or whether contemporary or traditional homes will be the favorite on any given day. The agent should also share data on how many homes have sold in your area in recent months and how long they were on the market, so that your expectations aren't unreasonable.

If you are in a financial bind or in a hurry, you'll also want to let the agent know generally, but you don't need to show your whole hand. You want the agent to try to get a good deal for you, rather than to sell the house quickly at almost any price. Keep in mind that the agent must sell the home to get paid, even if it's at a reduced price. As an added incentive, you might want to offer a bonus if the house is sold above a certain price within thirty days, or if you get your asking price.

IF YOU ARE IN A FINANCIAL BIND

Since 2008 about 1.5 million homes have been foreclosed on by banks, and many other owners have fallen behind on their house payments, often on homes that are now worth less than the mortgage on them. Billions of dollars in home values have simply disappeared.

But for all that, trying to keep a house that is too expensive for you or a home that has fallen in value below the mortgage amount still is a very complex and painful experience. If you're really struggling to make ends meet, the idea that you can mail in your keys to the lender and get out of your debt may sound appealing, but in reality, it is far less than that.

As mentioned in Chapter 5, a foreclosure or a short sale can stain your credit report for seven years and reduce your credit score for three to seven years, depending on how high your score was before. If you value your current credit score and the flexibility it gives you, you'll want to avoid these moves if possible. You'll also want to keep up your mortgage payments if you can. As previously noted, being thirty days late on one mortgage payment can knock up to a hundred points off an excellent credit score, meaning you'll pay much more for credit and you may have less available.

However, if you've lost your job or your family has lost a wage earner and your home's value has plunged, you may need to find other options—and there are many possible options to explore.

If you lose a job or a wage earner and find yourself in a financial bind, call your lender right away and try to work out a plan or buy some time, following up weekly until the situation is resolved. Lenders, the federal government, and many states have programs that may help you.

In 2011, many lenders were still wrestling with loads of foreclosures and they weren't moving especially fast. Borrowers and housing counselors complain that banks still lose an alarming amount of paperwork, make inconsistent decisions, and can be painfully slow to make up their minds. But because of the high demand, they all have departments charged with working on problem loans and some may be willing to work with you to try to keep you in the house, either by reducing your interest rate, stretching out your loan, or even forgiving part of it. To the degree you can, try to keep paying the mortgage at least for a while to give yourself more time to work on a solution.

If you want some assistance in the process, you can schedule a free counseling session with a HUD-approved housing counselor, who can help you assess your situation and may be able to cut through some of the red tape. Go to HUD.gov and click on "Avoid a foreclosure" or "Talk to a housing counselor." Often, the same nonprofit firms that offer credit counseling and mandatory bankruptcy counseling also have experts on your housing options and how to most effectively negotiate with your lender. Unfortunately, some scammers try to convince people to pay for help negotiating with lenders. Note that the services of HUD counselors are free and you shouldn't pay for that kind of help.

Following are the most common options.

A temporary modification or forbearance. If you have lost a job or if you're trying to decide what to do, you can ask your lender for a temporary modification to your loan terms. The lender may be willing to let you skip some payments or reduce your payment for three to six months while you work to get back on your feet. Sometimes the temporary fixes can be extended for a few more months, but beyond that you'll need a more permanent solution.

You'll still owe the amount that you didn't pay, so be sure you understand what happens when the temporary period is over. Some lenders may add the extra amount you owe to the end of your mortgage, but others may expect you to pay it back in a lump sum almost as soon as the forbearance period ends.

Permanent modification. If you can no longer make your mortgage payment because it's simply too high or you've taken a pay cut, a government program called Home Affordable Modification Program, or HAMP, is intended to encourage lenders to consider a permanent modification. In addition, many banks have their own modification programs.

To qualify for the government program, the house must be your primary residence and you must have gotten your mortgage before January 1, 2009. You'll have to prove that you have the income to pay at least some of the mortgage but that you have a financial hardship that makes paying the current loan difficult; it's not enough to complain that your home value has fallen or the loan is expensive.

If all goes well, the lender will consider cutting your interest rate to as low as 2 percent, with the goal of reducing your payment to 31 percent of your monthly total income. If that isn't enough, the lender may also extend the loan out to as long as forty years.

If neither of those gets your payment low enough for you to afford it, then the modification program won't be a possibility. A housing counselor can help you figure that out before you go to the trouble of trying to work with your lender and may be able to work with you and the lender to make the transaction happen.

The reductions may not be truly permanent. After five years, your interest rate may slowly creep up again until it reaches the market rate at the time that the loan was restructured.

If you think you'll qualify for it, try to temper your expectations. Counselors say that some transactions can happen in thirty days, some take months, and some, for unknown reasons, never go through. If you have a second loan or a home equity loan, the transaction will be more difficult.

There are other programs for modifying second mortgages and even a program that runs through 2012 to encourage lenders to consider actually reducing some mortgage balances—but housing counselors said in 2011 that such a step was extremely rare. More information is at MakingHome Affordable.gov.

A short sale. If you aren't going to be able to continue to make your payments and your home has fallen in value, one of your best options is to try to find a buyer and then ask the lender to approve a short sale, selling the property for less than what you owe without you having to come up with the balance.

Lenders have an incentive to see houses sold to new buyers rather than taking possession themselves, especially in some troubled markets where they may already own more homes than they want. This isn't a quick process: in addition to listing the home for sale and finding a buyer, you'll need to get the right person at your lending institution to sign off on the sales price, a process that can drag on for months. The tortoiselike nature of the sale may test your patience, your agent's, and your buyer's, sometimes to the point that the buyer will simply give up.

In addition, under the laws of most states, the lender could come after you for the difference between the sale price and the loan value, especially if it believes you have substantial assets. Luckily, that seldom happens these days, given how many homes lenders have to worry about.

In normal times, you also would be taking on a big potential tax bill. Typically, the Internal Revenue Service treats debt forgiveness as income, regardless of whether the debt is credit card related or a mortgage. So if you failed to pay off part of the debt through a short sale or the bank took over the whole debt, you might have to pay income taxes on the amount that you didn't pay. However, the Mortgage Forgiveness Debt Relief Act of 2007 allows taxpayers to avoid paying such taxes on mortgage debt forgiveness up to $2 million on their primary residence through 2012 if the reason was directly related to a decline in the home's value or the owner's financial situation. What happens after 2012 will depend on Congress.

Deed-in-lieu-of-foreclosure. If you can no longer make your payments and want to make a graceful exit, your lender may allow you to voluntarily turn your keys over to the bank, skipping the long and painful legal process that often goes with a foreclosure. In reality, however, this option doesn't happen very often.

Usually, you'll need to spend at least three months trying to sell the house before the lender will agree to this method. There's even a government program called Home Affordable Foreclosure Alternatives to support people who take this avenue. Under that program, lenders release the borrower from all further liability and the borrower may be eligible for up to $3,000 in relocation assistance. Some states may also have special programs to help troubled homeowners.

PROTECTING YOUR FUTURE

If you know you are likely to take a hit to your credit from a short sale or a foreclosure, start looking for a rental or another place to live *before* the transactions are under way. You'll also need to save up to make deposits, such as enough to pay the first and last months' rent.

This is a tricky situation—especially since it involves spending that all-important cash—but you need to protect yourself and your family. For one, you'll want the security of knowing where you're going to live before you actually have to give up your current house. In addition, landlords may not be willing to rent to people with troubled credit or they may demand much larger deposits or more income than they would otherwise. Once a short sale or foreclosure shows up on your credit report, everything may get more expensive, from rent to lining up new utilities.

(In communities where home prices have plummeted, some devious homeowners have even purchased a new home at a lower price before giving up a home that has fallen in value to foreclosure—but that's pushing the envelope. Though lenders may be too busy to pursue it these days, in most states, they can go after people who walk away from debts and who have the ability to pay. That kind of tactic may work but it's hardly the best game plan.)

BUY OR RENT?

Once you've made the decision to move, your next consideration is whether to buy or rent. Although you may not feel certain, either is a perfectly good option that comes with some real pluses and minuses.

Home ownership is often touted for providing safe and stable neighborhoods and allowing owners to build equity in a home. But as you already know, it's wickedly expensive, requiring a sizable down payment, ongoing maintenance, taxes, and sometimes homeowners dues or condo maintenance fees. In addition, the fickle nature of home markets means that you shouldn't buy a house that you don't plan to own for at least five years—something that can be hard to predict if you're still in the throes of a financial or personal setback. The way prices can fluctuate means that you can lose a lot of money in the short term. The way mortgages are structured (you pay mostly interest at the beginning and mostly principal at the end), you won't really start to build equity for a few years. Owning your home for at least five years gives housing markets time to recover or climb and affords you some time for starting to pay down some of the loan.

Renters, by contrast, get to turn over most of the headaches of home ownership to the landlord, who is responsible for maintenance, upkeep, taxes, and other costs. Because most leases run for just a year, you have more flexibility if a job opportunity or family situation requires you to relocate. In addition, if you're new to a community, renting gives you time to get to know different neighborhoods, traffic patterns, and pricing before you settle on an area to buy in.

In both cases, the same rules of thumb about what you can afford apply, though with renting you don't need to include property taxes. Still, rent or own, you shouldn't spend more than about a third of your gross pay on housing, or have home costs and other debts that add up to more than 36 percent of your total income.

SIGNING A LEASE

Leases, like all contracts, can seem like a long list of legalese. But as with most contracts, you'll want to know exactly what you're getting into—and maybe more important, how you can get out of it if you need to. However painful it may be, you need to read the fine print or enlist someone you trust to read it for you.

You'll almost certainly be asked to put down a deposit, which can be as little as part of a month's rent to as much as the first and last months of rent. The lease should spell out how and when you may get that deposit back. In addition, it will detail how long the rental agreement lasts, when the rent is due, and what the penalty is if you are late. Other things to look for are as follows:

- When the lease expires, do you go month to month or must you renew the lease?

- Under what circumstances can the landlord raise the rent?

- What's included in the lease in terms of appliances, utilities, parking, and other amenities?

- How are repairs handled? Who is responsible for pest control?

- How can the landlord terminate the lease? How can you end the lease if you need to move? Can you sublet the place to someone else?

Before you move in, walk through with the landlord, noting any problems. Or take photos with a time stamp to verify any maintenance issues. Those may be important when it comes time to get your security deposit back.

RENTERS' INSURANCE

If you own clothes, furniture, a laptop or two, or other possessions that would be pricey to replace if they were damaged or stolen, you need renters' insurance. True, you won't be responsible if the structure is damaged. But a fire or an overflowing bathtub can cause real damage to your stuff and theft is a risk anywhere.

As insurance goes, renters' insurance is one of the cheapest, usually costing less than $300 a year. You can keep the price down by choosing a higher deductible, like $500 per claim instead of $250.

Although you can shop around, it may be easiest to simply get renters' insurance at the same place you get car insurance; in fact, you may get a discount for having more than one kind of insurance.

In addition to the cost and the deductible, here are other things to consider:

- Can you get insurance for replacement cost, instead of actual value? Your laptop may be worth $100 now, but you'll have to pay much more to replace it.

- How are electronics, jewelry, fine art, and other pricey items covered? If the coverage isn't adequate, you may want to insure those separately.

- Are your personal items covered when you travel?

- Are there exclusions, like for earthquake damage? If you can't stay in your apartment, will the insurance cover the cost of a hotel or temporary housing?

- Will you have liability coverage if something happens to someone while they are in your apartment?

Buying other kinds of insurance, including homeowners insurance, is covered in Chapter 8.

CHOOSING YOUR NEW HOME

Finally, a few considerations apply when choosing a place to relocate, regardless of whether you buy or rent:

- Check out the neighborhood thoroughly, visiting both during the day and at night, on weekends and weekdays. You'll want to be sure you feel safe at any time.

- Chat with neighbors about what they like and don't like about the area. You'll learn much more from people who live there than you will from real estate or apartment-leasing agents.

- Before you buy a home, you should have a professional inspector walk through and check out all the systems—plumbing, heating and air-conditioning, and electrical—as well as the roof, foundation, and general construction quality. Although rental inspections generally are much less formal, it doesn't hurt to bring along a friend who is knowledgeable about real estate and construction. Many landlords may dress up a place with fresh paint or new countertops or floors, but ignore growing mold, leaky air-conditioning systems, or drafty windows. Even new construction can be flawed.

- Just as you will compare recent home sales in your area before bidding on a house, you should compare rental prices in an area as well. Typically, both rents and sales are based on pricing per square foot of living space, with new or renovated spaces costing more than dated ones.

- In both renting and home buying, just about everything is negotiable, from the price to whether certain appliances, furniture, or window coverings are included. When you agree on something, be sure to put it in writing in the lease or sales agreement or as an addendum. It's very hard to go back after the fact to claim something that was agreed to with only a handshake.

CHAPTER 7

NAVIGATING THE BIG "C" EXPENSES: CARS AND COLLEGE

Managing your finances would be so much easier if most of your expenses were simple and regular, like paying for housing, utilities, and food. Once you got into a routine, all you'd have to worry about would be the monthly bills and savings for retirement.

But, of course, life isn't nearly that neat and tidy, as you well know by now. To stay out of debt and truly live within your means, you always need to be thinking ahead. You always need to be putting away cash for various big-ticket items, like vacations, furniture, or holiday presents.

Then there are the *really* big expenses that come along, most notably cars, and if you have kids, college. The cost of both can be shockingly high, and the only way you may be able to afford them is to borrow and pay for them over a number of years. But if you plan ahead and set reasonable expectations, you can lessen the blow—and the debt you take on.

THE CAR CHASE

No doubt, Americans love their cars. We love new cars, and we love replacing our cars every few years. But if you buy a new car every three or four years or lease cars so that you can always have one of the newest models, you'll be throwing money away. After all, cars are not assets that can appreciate in value, like a home can. In fact, every day, they *decrease* a little bit in value. Spending on a nice car is okay if you have the money to burn, but if your budget is tight or you have other goals, there are much better ways to manage your wheels and the expenses that go with it.

This can feel like a painful comeuppance if you see your car as a status symbol and worry that trading it in for a cheaper model will make you look like a failure. But in truth, people who make practical and careful choices about their cars are clever and smart because they're putting their money to its best use and retaining the rest for things that they will enjoy even more.

When you choose a car, what really matters isn't the age of a car or the name on the rear, but whether the car is reliable enough that it gets you safely to work, to the store, and through all the car pools that you need it to. If your car is fitting that bill, try to put away the urge to trade it in for a newer model and plan on driving it for a total of seven to ten years, or until it crosses 100,000 miles. If your wheels have grown unreliable, however, it may be time to make a change. You won't get very far if your car is always in the shop, draining your budget with repairs.

When deciding what kind of car to buy, be honest about your needs and consider the following:

- True, the Mini Cooper and Volkswagen Beetle are adorable, but if you're going to be carting around several large teenagers, they won't handle the job. Consider whether you need two doors or four, and whether you'll need a big trunk, a hatchback, or all-wheel drive.

- Any car should be both reliable and safe. You can look up government safety ratings at SaferCar.gov. *Consumer Reports* and J.D. Power are both known for their car reliability surveys, which you can access online.

- With oil prices bouncing up and down, fuel efficiency is going to continue to be important. Gasoline prices may bounce around some, but they aren't likely to be terribly cheap—and you don't want price spikes to squeeze your budget any more than necessary. Just as you have to consider utility costs when you buy a home, weigh what your monthly gasoline bill might be when you're looking at buying a potential gas guzzler.

- If you have your heart set on a particular car that will stretch your budget, consider buying a used version that is two to four years old, preferably with relatively low miles, instead of a brand-new one. Some used cars are still under warranty, and many car dealers offer certified used cars that have been inspected and repaired and come with a warranty. They may cost a bit more than similar used cars, but there's a value in knowing that any troublesome problems should be covered.

- Try to buy off season. Convertibles are cheaper in the winter and all-wheel-drive vehicles are cheaper in the spring and summer. As new models begin to show up, last year's models decrease in price. In addition, car dealers may have more incentive to negotiate toward the end of the month, when they're trying to make their sales goals.

- Before you even start shopping, figure out what you can fit in your budget and how you can make it work. If you'll be trading in a car, research that car's value online, using

KBB.com (Kelley Blue Book), Edmunds.com, the Yahoo! cars site, or even by reading the ads in your local paper. You'll need cash for a down payment, preferably 20 percent or more. The more you have, the less pressure the purchase will put on your monthly expenses. The sites also can show you any incentives that dealers have available at the moment. Once you figure out how large a payment you can afford, you can use the calculators at those sites to figure out roughly how much you can afford to spend. Then you'll be ready to start test-driving cars.

BUYING AND FINANCING A CAR

Everyone you talk to about a car will probably focus on the monthly payment. That's what the car salespeople want you to think about—because then you won't focus on the purchase price or the interest rate they're offering you.

In fact, one of the most common sales pitches is to try to get you to lease a car for three or four years rather than buy one. Because the monthly rates appear very cheap, this can look like a good deal. But intuitively, you should know dealers wouldn't offer it if they weren't making a bunch of money off you. In addition to monthly payments, the lease will include a decent down payment and some fees built in—and at the end of the lease, you won't have anything to show for your payments. If you buy a car, finance it for three or four years, and then continue to drive it for another five or six years, you'll have years to pay yourself to rebuild a car-savings account—so much so that someday, you may find yourself paying cash for all your cars and skipping car loans altogether.

If you're going to finance the car purchase, you'll want to zero in on the total cost: How much will you be paying for the car and how much will the interest add to your total outlay? (It's a simple calculation: multiply your payment times the number of months and add in your down payment, taxes, and any trade-in value.) The whole shebang is probably a very big number, and paying close attention to that will help you get a much better deal.

Once you settle on the car you want, gather information online about what it should really cost you. If you're going to be financing the purchase, you'll need to know your credit score so that you know if you'll qualify for the best interest rates.

Shop the interest rates at a couple of local banks or credit unions and try to get preapproved for a three- or four-year loan, so that you'll be certain to have financing. If you can make the payment only if you get a five- or six-year loan, you probably can't afford the car and you'll be taking a fair bit of risk. If something happens to the car in year five or six, you could end up owing more than the car is worth.

Unless you're very good at negotiating, don't start your negotiations in the car dealership. Instead, go home and e-mail the dealers in your area, asking for specific quotes on the model, color, and features you want. Internet sales teams often will come back with much more competitive prices than you might get in person, partly because they know that people who shop online aggressively compare prices. Stick to your guns and don't pay for add-ons that you don't need or can't afford, whether it's extra-large floor mats, pinstripes, or a moonroof.

Only after you have the best prices in hand for the vehicle you want should you go to close the deal in person. Don't discuss the trade-in or the financing until you've agreed on a price for the car. Dealers may offer you a seemingly terrific price, and then hike your interest rate to make up for it. You want a good deal on each part of the purchase—the price, the trade-in, and the interest rate—and should handle each of them separately.

If the dealer is offering special incentives, run the numbers through an online calculator to be sure you get the best deal. In 2011, Toyota dealers were offering $2,000 cash back or 0 percent financing on the popular Camry. Surprisingly, for someone who qualified for the best interest rates, the monthly payment at 0 percent was actually about $10 higher than the payment if the buyer got $2,000 in cash back and paid 4 percent in interest.

IF YOU ARE IN A FINANCIAL BIND

If you have lost your job or suffered a financial setback and cannot make your car payment, call the lender and discuss your situation. Some lenders may waive your payment for thirty days or propose other options. While it may be painful to address the problem, it's better than having a lender call and harass you about a payment or show up in your driveway to repossess your car.

As with other debts, you have a few options:

- Depending on your credit score and payment history, you may be able to refinance the loan to the current rates today. Or you may find that your best alternative is to pay a higher interest rate but over a longer period of time, which would reduce your monthly payment.

- You don't have to rely on your current lender to refinance the loan. Check with your bank or credit union to see if it can make you a new, affordable loan that would allow you to pay off the old loan. You likely will get the best deal at a place where you already have accounts, but try at least two or three lenders.

- You could sell the car and use the proceeds to repay the loan. If your car is worth less than your loan, however, you'll have to pay the difference. And you'll also have to figure out how to pay for new, presumably much-cheaper transportation.

- If at all possible, you want to avoid having your car repossessed or turning a car back to the lender. Both will be treated as defaults on your credit record, which will limit your ability to borrow in the future and will cost you higher interest rates for some years. In addition, if your car is worth less than you owe, you'll still be on the hook for the difference, meaning you still may be paying for a car that you don't own.

The potential for that kind of trouble is yet another reason to take the conservative road in choosing your wheels, leaning toward what's practical and useful rather than stretching for something fancy and impressive.

COPING WITH COLLEGE COSTS

While you will drive several cars in a financial lifetime, luckily you'll only have to deal with college once per child—though that's hardly consoling, given how expensive it is. According to the College Board, average tuition, fees, and room and board at a four-year public college was more than $16,000 in 2011 for in-state students. The cost to attend an out-of-state public school is nearing $30,000, and the average private university is around $37,000. If you have the Ivy League or another prestigious institution in mind, the full cost has crossed $50,000 a year.

Daunting, isn't it? But as outrageous as it sounds, it's not impossible. Many, many students receive financial aid—an average of about $6,000 a year at public schools and $16,000 at private schools. Some colleges and universities have made a conscious effort to reduce the amount of debt that young people and their families must take on. Although there is no hard and fast rule, many students from families whose income is less than $100,000 will qualify for some kind of need-based aid, and students from some families with income as high as $200,000 may qualify under certain circumstances.

FINANCIAL AID

If you have lost a job or your family income has dropped because of a divorce or the death of a spouse, you probably will want to take a close look at your child's financial aid options. If you student is already in school, he or she should visit the financial aid office, which should have procedures for addressing a change in the student's circumstances. In many cases, at least some aid is available to students who qualify.

If your student hasn't started college yet, entire books and websites are available to help you through the financial-aid maze once you're ready. But to give you a head start, here's a rundown of the basics of getting help with college, in the order you want to pursue them.

FAFSA. The road to any kind of financial help starts with the FAFSA form, the Free Application for Federal Student Aid. Please note that it's *free*! You should never have to pay anyone or give a credit card to begin this process. To fill out the FAFSA form, you will need tax records, bank statements, and other information, which is detailed at Fafsa.gov. There is also a Fafsa4caster, which can estimate whether you qualify for aid and what kind.

You'll have to apply for financial aid every year in order to receive it. The schools you apply to may also require separate financial aid forms.

If you are divorced, one parent or the other must fill out the form. Generally, the parent of the household where the child spends the most time does this; if the child spends the same amount of time with both parents, then the parent that provides the most financial support fills out the form. If a widowed or divorced parent has remarried, then the stepparent's financial information must be included to accurately depict the family's financial situation.

Grants. Government grants go to students with the greatest need, generally those whose family income is below $50,000 a year. The biggest such programs are the federal Pell grants, which provide up to $5,500 a year in grants that don't have to be repaid. The amount paid is supposed to go up gradually over the next few years—but Congress has also considered cutting the grants in the wake of increased demand.

Scholarships. Many colleges, companies, organizations, and others give scholarship money to people who can show a need. Websites like FastWeb.com list all kinds of scholarships that are available to all kinds of students. A number of schools also give merit scholarships, or funds based on a student's academic or other talents rather than the student's finances. Students who qualify as National Merit finalists, based on the National Merit Scholarship Qualifying Test given each October, also may qualify for large (and sometimes full) scholarships. If your student makes outstanding grades or has a special skill, it's worth investigating what kinds of scholarship money may be available.

Work-study. Students who qualify for financial aid typically are expected to work during the school year at on-campus jobs, which pay at least the federal minimum wage. How much the student is expected to earn during the school year and in the summer will be spelled out by the financial aid office, which also will provide leads on campus jobs. (Wages go to the student to be used for living or other costs.) Students who don't receive financial aid can get campus or off-campus jobs to help defray college costs.

Subsidized loans. The federal government has several loan programs for students and parents that vary depending on financial need. *Perkins loans* of up to $5,500 a year are awarded to students with the most financial need and are paid back at 5 percent interest over ten years. *Stafford loans* for students with financial need carry an interest rate of 3.4 percent for those disbursed before July 1, 2012. That rate is scheduled to climb to 6.8 percent for those disbursed after that date. In both cases, the government pays the interest while the student is in college and then the student must pay it when the loan payments start a few months after graduation. Stafford loans are repaid in ten to twenty-five years.

Government aid is paid to the school's financial aid office, where it is applied first to tuition, fees, and room and board. Money left over is given to the student for other expenses.

Other loans. Students who fill out the FAFSA but who don't have a demonstrated need can get *unsubsidized Stafford loans*, which carry interest rates of 6.8 percent and can be repaid over ten to twenty-five years. The amount a dependent student can borrow each year ranges from $3,500 to $5,500. Interest is owed right away, but students can postpone it, adding it to the loan balance and starting payments after graduation.

Parents with a decent credit record can borrow under the government's *PLUS loan* program, which charges an interest rate of 7.9 percent. Those who have an "adverse credit history"—which can include being 90 days or more late on a debt payment, giving up a house to foreclosure, or filing for bankruptcy—won't qualify. In those cases, students can borrow more money (up to a limit set by the government) under the unsubsidized Stafford loan program.

Under new rules put in place in 2010, all the government loans are made directly by the US Department of Education. College financial aid offices can provide more information.

For many families, these programs still don't begin to provide enough help to cover the rising cost of college. Families with home equity may find it makes sense to refinance their mortgage and take cash out to help with college costs—but only if the new payment isn't burdensome and some equity still remains. This should be done judiciously, since you're essentially betting your house if you can't pay the new mortgage.

The last resort should be private loans from banks and credit unions, which often carry much higher interest rates and fees. Since rates will vary, shop around before signing up.

Although a college education is an experience that pays off for a lifetime, it doesn't have to leave you and your child in a lifetime of debt. As a rule of thumb, undergraduates shouldn't borrow more than they would earn in their first year out of school. So future schoolteachers should limit their total loans to about $30,000. Future engineers may be able to borrow more. But generally, total debt should remain below $40,000. If the school is simply too expensive to do that, then the family should question whether that's the best option.

SAVING FOR COLLEGE

All of this financial aid detail may seem irrelevant if your children are young. After all, you are years from knowing their interests, never mind their grades and SAT scores. But the day will come soon enough, and you should start planning early because how you save for their education could affect their chances of getting financial aid later. So if you think your children may be candidates for need-based aid down the road, you'll want to take steps early on to keep from accumulating too much in assets in their own names.

Saving for a child's college education is difficult. At the stage that most people have children, they're also buying a first home; feeding, clothing, and caring for a child and any siblings; and trying to build a career. At the same time, they should be saving for retirement—in fact, that should be a priority—because you can borrow for college, but you can't borrow your way through retirement. Only the most careful planners (or the wealthiest) have funds left over to put aside for a college education. Still, every little bit will help when the day comes.

Here are common ways to save for college, with some of the pros and cons.

529 plans. Nearly every state offers at least one 529 college-savings plan, and some states offer several. There are plans that you can enroll in individually, and plans designed for financial advisers that typically require you to pay higher fees and expenses.

The plans come with special tax advantages, though you do not get a tax break on your deductions like you do with retirement accounts. However, your investments can grow tax-deferred and if you use the funds to pay for college, you won't have to pay federal taxes on your gains. Many states also offer state-tax breaks for residents, which can range from modest to substantial, and a few states offer special incentives, such as matching some of your investments.

Even though you're saving for a specific child, the 529 plan is counted in the parents' assets when the student applies for financial aid. That means that only 5.64 percent of the amount in the fund will be counted when assessing whether the student qualifies for financial aid.

As with retirement plans, many 529 plans offer many investment options. In fact, there are literally thousands of choices. Most plans allow you to simply pick a fund based on your child's age. When your child is young, that fund will take more risk, investing heavily in stocks. As your child nears college age, that fund should grow more conservative, increasing the allocation to cash and bonds and decreasing the percentage invested in stocks.

However, the proportions vary wildly among plans, and when the stock market plunged in 2008–09, many parents were shocked to see their teenagers' college savings dive along with it. If you take this route, you should know about how much of your money will be invested in stocks each year. In many plans, you can choose between conservative, moderate, and aggressive portfolios. You can also skip the prefabricated funds and pick your investments from a menu of funds, which should include low-cost index funds. (See Chapter 9, "Managing Your Money for the Long Term.")

A number of states originally offered "prepaid" tuition plans, in which your investment covered tuition at your state schools some years in the future, no matter how much tuition increased. In the early days of 529 plans, those options appeared to be a great deal—and unfortunately, they were a bit too great. Tuition costs kept growing, especially as states struggled with financial challenges, and investment returns didn't keep up, meaning that a number of these prepaid plans didn't have enough assets to cover their commitments. Some stopped accepting new participants, and a few were retooled.

In 2011, Florida, Illinois, Maryland, Massachusetts, Michigan, Mississippi, Nevada, Pennsylvania, Texas, Virginia, and Washington still offered prepaid plans. Some of the states back the programs if investments fall short or consider other steps to ensure participants get a fair deal, while others don't. If your child doesn't go to an in-state public school, you can get a refund, but it may not include investment gains. If you're interested in that type of plan, read the plan's details carefully.

In a similar vein, if you think your child will go to a private college, the Private College 529 allows you to buy tuition certificates in today's dollars that can be used toward tuition in the future at more than 270 private schools. You can learn more at PrivateCollege529.com.

Because 529 plans lock up funds for college and provide tax breaks, they are one of the most recommended ways to save for higher education. But there are other things you should know:

- Funds in a 529 plan must be used for higher education. If your child finds that college isn't for him or ends up with a lucrative scholarship that pays her way, you can change the beneficiary on the account to another child, a niece or nephew, or even yourself. But if you use the funds for something other than higher education, you will pay a tax penalty.

- You can change your investment selection only once a year. So if you reevaluate your account every January, and something happens in August that makes you want to take a different strategy, you'll be out of luck.

- 529 plans make the most sense for people who start saving early, because the investments will have the longest amount of time to grow. Realistically, college funds have, at most, about twenty years to grow. But if you wait until your child is twelve to start an account and the stock market has some rotten years, your investments may fall in value or go sideways, negating any potential tax benefits. If you don't start saving before your child is ten years old, you might do just as well saving outside a 529 account.

- 529 plans also make a lot of sense for people who plan to save a lot. Rules vary by state, but some plans allow you to save more than $200,000 per child—keeping in mind that all the money must go toward education. You or a grandparent can even make a large lump sum gift of up to $65,000 (equal to five years' worth of gifts allowed under IRS rules), which can then grow tax-free. The more you save, the more valuable the tax savings are. If you're putting away only $1,000 a year, your tax savings may not be worth the hassle of choosing and monitoring an account. You might be just as well off investing the funds in a low-cost index mutual fund.

- As with other investments, fees really can have an impact on your final savings. Morningstar.com and Savingforcollege .com are two good websites for finding the lowest-cost plans and seeing where your state's plan ranks.

Though 529 plans are heavily marketed and are a great option for many people, the restrictions mean they aren't for everyone.

Coverdell education savings accounts. These accounts can be more limited than 529s in some ways, and more flexible in others.

Unlike a 529 plan, you can invest a maximum of $2,000 a year in a Coverdell account, so these are best for people who don't want to put a lot away in a tax-advantaged plan. In addition, there are income restrictions on who can contribute: adjusted gross income in 2011 couldn't exceed $220,000 for married couples filing jointly or $110,000 for single filers.

While 529 plans are only for higher education, money in Coverdell accounts can be used for elementary and secondary school as well.

Most 529 accounts come with limited choices of investments selected by the plan administrators. But a Coverdell account can be invested in just about anything you can buy in a brokerage account—stocks, bonds, mutual funds, ETFs, or even certificates of deposit. That investment flexibility is one of the biggest attractions.

As with 529s, accounts in the parents' names are considered the parents' assets, so they won't have much effect on the students' chances for financial aid. The money must be used for qualified education expenses and it must be spent by the time the child turns thirty. Parents and grandparents can contribute to both a Coverdell and a 529 plan, keeping in mind that the IRS has different rules for annual gifts of more than $13,000 per person or $26,000 per couple.

After 2012, the maximum contribution to a Coverdell account is scheduled to drop to $500 a year, unless Congress extends the $2,000 contribution.

Other ways to save. If you're late getting started or if you know that your child isn't likely to qualify for financial aid, you have other options.

- *Regular savings.* The most common way people save for college is in plain old savings accounts. If you aren't sure you want to lock up your money solely for education or if you don't have a long time until Junior heads out the door, you could simply save in your own accounts in whatever ways make you comfortable—an online savings account, certificates of deposit, mutual funds, or bonds set to mature around the time the college costs will start. You won't get the tax benefits of a 529, but you won't have the hassle of choosing a plan and you won't have restrictions on how you spend the money.

- *UGMAs and UTMAs.* Under the Uniform Gift to Minors Act and the Uniform Transfers to Minors Act, you can make investments in the child's name that will become your child's property at either eighteen or twenty-one, depending on your state laws. That means your adult children can spend the money however they like—on education, a first car or home, or to live as a ski bum in Colorado. These accounts make sense only if you're fairly certain your kiddo won't qualify for financial aid. In assessing financial need, financial aid formulas count 20 percent of the assets in the child's name, while including only about 5.6 percent of the parents' assets.

    The real advantage of these accounts used to be the way they were taxed. The first $950 of earned income is exempt from taxes and the next $950 is taxed at the child's rate. For many years, the income over $1,900 was taxed at the higher of the child's rate or your rate until the child reached age fourteen, and then it was taxed at the child's rate. Now, however, income over $1,900 will be taxed at your higher rate until the child turns nineteen—or even twenty-four if he or she is a full-time student—negating many of the tax benefits. Once the money is given away, it can't be taken back.

- *Roth IRAs.* Some parents and financial advisers have used Roth IRAs as a potential way to save for college, even though they are designed for retirement. You can put up to $5,000 a year of after-tax money in a Roth IRA, if your income isn't too high, and the money can grow tax-deferred. Because you've already paid taxes on your contributions, you can withdraw them at any time, leaving the investment gains. If you don't need the money for college, you can still use it for your retirement. More information on Roth IRAs is in Chapter 9.

- *Community college.* Community college isn't a savings account, of course, but it's certainly a cheaper way to start college. Tuition often runs in the hundreds of dollars instead of the thousands and it can be an effective way to get your basic courses out of the way. Many big private and public universities have programs for accepting transfer students who have made high grades at nearby community colleges, and sometimes they offer scholarship funds. For a family facing other financial challenges, community college can be a great way to begin an education without adding substantial stress to the budget.

CHAPTER 8

Shoring Up Your Insurance

Insurance sometimes feels like the dust bunnies collecting under the dining room table. It's too important to ignore, but not important enough to want to invest much time thinking about it.

As you restart your financial life, however, you'll want to take a look at all your insurance coverage, to review whether it's adequate or whether you even need it given your changed circumstances, and to be sure you are paying a fair price. After all, insurance is a big budget item, a notable chunk out of the checking account. If you choose properly, though, good insurance coverage will protect you when you most need it and allow you to spend more of your precious time worrying about other things—like housework.

As with any big purchase, you will find it worth your while to shop around for the best deals. Prices, or the *premiums* you pay, may vary widely. Of course, the amount of coverage you want will affect the price as will the deductible, or the amount you must pay before the insurance kicks in. States have varying insurance regulations, and your insurance rates will reflect those quirks, as well as each company's claims experience and its own method for weighing its risk. In addition, more and more insurers use credit histories and credit scores in determining how much they will charge for homeowners and auto policies, saying that certain behaviors, such as missed bill payments, raise the risk that someone will file more insurance claims.

There isn't a single insurance score in the industry that is widely used like the FICO score for mortgages and credit cards. Several firms sell so-called credit-based insurance scores and some insurance companies check credit records and calculate their own scores. Insurers have to tell you if your rates are being increased because of credit issues. But when you are comparing prices, it can be hard to tell how much your credit history affects your rates, unless you ask and the company is forthcoming. Some companies rely much more heavily on credit information than others, and if your record is less than stellar, you should look for a company that puts less emphasis on that and more on other factors.

If you have filed for bankruptcy, your insurance company may continue to renew your policies as long as you continue to pay your premiums, but your premiums may go up because of the blemish on your credit record. Or you could get a notice that the company won't be renewing your insurance. In that case, of course, you'll have to shop around to see what options are available to you. If you need car insurance, your last resort may be your state's high-risk pool.

The use of credit scores has been controversial. Some consumer advocates argue that your credit history should be irrelevant in an insurance decision, and some state legislatures have banned or limited the use of them. (In California, for instance, credit scores can't be used in determining auto insurance.) Your state insurance department website should offer detailed information about auto insurers, including whether credit history is a factor in your rates.

Other insurance-cost issues to keep in mind include the following:

- Many insurance companies offer a discount to customers who buy multiple policies, like auto, homeowners, and life insurance. It's worth asking about such discounts if you are comparing prices on several insurance products.

- Loyalty also matters. You may earn special discounts if you have been with a company for five years or more. That shouldn't stop you from looking for better prices every few years, however, since you may do better with another company.

- When you're shopping, check both insurance agents and companies that sell directly to consumers. While agents receive a commission, they aren't always more expensive.

- You may receive additional discounts if you agree to give up paper bills or if your payments are automatically deducted from your checking account. There may also be a discount if you pay in full, rather than monthly. (Be aware that some companies may bill you only four months out of every six for auto insurance; you may want to set aside money every month so that you aren't surprised when the bills restart after a couple of months.)

- Think hard before you file small claims, since insurance companies track how many claims you file and even a single one can increase your premiums. Instead, try to live with a dent in the fender or pay for small repairs out of your own pocket, saving your calls to the insurance company for the truly big problems.

- If you have lost your job or are otherwise in financial distress, you will still need to keep paying insurance premiums to keep the insurance in force. Your policy will explain whether your insurance will lapse immediately when you miss a premium or whether the company must notify you first and give you an opportunity to get current. It may be helpful to speak with the insurer about your options, but unlike a credit card company, which may work with you so that it eventually gets paid, an insurance company doesn't have any reason to give you a free ride.

- While cost matters, so does service. Great prices are no help if the company doesn't respond to your calls or pay quickly. You can research complaints against a company on your state insurance department website or see whether an insurer has fewer or more complaints than average at the National Association of Insurance Commissioners site at http://eapps.naic.org/cis/.

There are many forms of insurance, some of which almost require an advanced degree to comprehend. But since your goal is to simplify and regenerate your financial life, not to complicate it, the focus here is on the most cost-efficient and plain-vanilla types of insurance.

CAR INSURANCE

If you have a car, you almost certainly have auto insurance, since nearly all states require it or require you to show proof of financial responsibility. But it can be a big cost, especially if there are multiple drivers in your house or if any of the drivers has had multiple accidents or tickets.

It's a good practice to review your coverage every two or three years, but especially when your circumstances change, to be sure you're getting the best rates available and that your coverage is adequate. A good policy not only protects you and your assets, but also ensures that you have the wheels you need to get to and from work.

How much insurance do you need? In most cases, the minimum required isn't enough. Many states require $25,000 in liability coverage for one person injured in an accident, $50,000 to cover all the injuries in an accident, and $10,000 to $25,000 to cover property damage. (This is displayed on policies as 25/50/10 or 25/50/25.)

But if you injure someone or are responsible for a multi-car accident and you don't have enough coverage, the injured parties may well hire a lawyer to sue you to make up the difference from your savings or other personal assets. Ideally, you'll carry at least $50,000 in injury coverage, $100,000 per accident, and enough to cover an expensive car if you were to total it. You'll need more if you have substantial assets.

Some states also require you to have insurance that covers your potential medical expenses from an accident and no-fault insurance, which requires your company to pay no matter who was at fault.

Though they aren't required, you will also want *collision* insurance, which covers your car if it is damaged in an accident, and *comprehensive* insurance, which covers theft of the car, a break-in, or weather damage. These will keep you moving, but you may want to skip them if your jalopy is worth so little—say, a few thousand dollars or less—that the cost of this insurance isn't worth it.

If you need to cut what you are paying for insurance, consider raising your deductible before you slash coverage. Often, replacing a $250 deductible with one of $500 or $1,000 can result in large savings. You may also get discounts if you don't drive the car very much, if it has safety or antitheft features, and if you have taken a defensive driving course. Students who are drivers may qualify for good-grade discounts, and you may get a discount on a car driven mostly by a student away at college.

If your budget is very tight, the minimum state requirements may be all you can afford right now and if so, they'll have to do. If you have more than one car, you may also want to consider parking a car to save money, insuring only the one that is being driven.

Not all policies cover you if you're renting a car, so you should ask. That way, you'll know whether to accept or decline the rental-car company's insurance.

HOMEOWNERS INSURANCE

You may think of your home's value based on its potential sale price, but insurers see a different number: the cost to rebuild your home if it is destroyed by fire or badly damaged by a tornado or other weather-related tragedy. That amount could be more or less than your home's value, depending on the home itself and where you live.

If you have recently taken full possession of your home because of a divorce or the loss of your spouse, if you've remodeled, or if you haven't looked at your insurance in some time, then you may want to be sure the insurance is up to date with construction costs in your area.

You should be sure your policy will pay to replace or repair the damage based on the replacement value, or the current cost of construction. However, if your home is insured for a lot less than the real replacement value, then you may have to come up with some of the money on your own. You can pay extra for a policy that extends the replacement value by some percentage above your insured value, hedging your bets if construction costs skyrocket. But you should also keep the value up to date, unless your policy is automatically adjusted for inflation.

If you have to live somewhere else after your home is damaged or destroyed, your insurance should cover that as well.

Traditional homeowners policies do not cover flood damage. If you live in an area that has the potential for flooding, you'll need to buy flood insurance through the federal government's program. Go to FloodSmart.gov for more information.

Your personal items should be insured for 50 percent to 70 percent of your home's value. So if your home is insured for $300,000, your personal property should be insured up to at least $150,000. That coverage should also be for the cost to replace the items, not their current value; that is, your furniture may be worth only $1,000 at a garage sale today, but it would cost several times that to replace those furnishings at a store.

The insurance company may have caps on what it will pay for jewelry, fine art, and other valuables. If so, those items should be covered by additional insurance solely for those items. If your possessions are stolen when you are traveling or even simply lost, your homeowners insurance should pay to replace them.

Your policy also will include liability insurance, covering the cost if someone is injured while at your home. If you have substantial assets, you may want to consider an umbrella policy. (See below.)

As with other kinds of insurance, you can save money by raising your deductible to the highest level where you feel comfortable. You may qualify for discounts if you have a security system, smoke detectors, fire extinguishers, or other safety items.

If your home is severely damaged or destroyed, you will need an inventory of what is in it. If you had to create something like that because of a divorce or to settle an estate, you may want to keep the information in a safe-deposit box or some other safe place. You may also want to periodically make a video of each room so that you have a record of your possessions.

AN UMBRELLA POLICY

If you have substantial assets from savings, life insurance, or a divorce settlement, that important nest egg could be vulnerable if the unthinkable happens—like you or a family member is responsible for a car accident that severely injures several people or someone is badly hurt at your home.

True, you have liability insurance as part of your auto and homeowners policies, but those may top out at $300,000 each, or maybe a bit more. That may not be nearly enough to cover the cost or damages if you are sued over an unfortunate event.

An umbrella policy provides additional liability insurance, often $1 million or more, to protect you and your assets once the auto or home insurance has been exhausted. The cost may be as little as a few hundred dollars, depending on where you live and how much you need, but it gives you protection from putting your life savings at risk.

LIFE INSURANCE

Whether you need life insurance and how much you need depends on your new situation and those who rely on your income or the work you do at home.

You most likely need life insurance if:

- you have dependent children.

- you provide support to parents, a sibling, or another family member.

- you have a spouse who doesn't work outside the home or who relies at least in part on you to pay for the house or maintain a certain lifestyle.

- you stay at home with children, providing services that someone else would have to pay for if you weren't around.

You may not need life insurance if:

- you are single and without children.

- you are a single parent and your assets are significant enough to provide for your adult or nearly adult children and their future needs if you were to die.

- you are near enough to retirement that you don't have major financial obligations to worry about.

- you are married and your spouse has enough income or your estate is large enough to provide an appropriate standard of living if one of you were to die.

What kind of insurance do you need? To keep your finances simple and your costs down, shop for *term life insurance,* which works much like auto or homeowners insurance; that is, you buy a certain amount of coverage and pay an annual premium for it. When you stop paying for the coverage, it goes away. (*Cash value insurance* has a savings-account piece to it and its value can grow—but it is also far more expensive and complex.)

Many companies provide some life insurance to their employees as part of their benefits, sometimes a flat amount and sometimes an amount based on your annual income. You may also be able to buy additional insurance for you or your spouse through your employer.

If you buy insurance from an agent or directly from an insurance company, you may be asked a lot of personal questions, including how much you drink and whether you have ever used illegal drugs. The policy can be invalidated if you are found to have lied about the answers, so be honest. Depending on how much insurance you want to buy, you may also have to submit to a blood test and a medical exam.

Your premium will be based on how risky the insurance company thinks you are, and you probably will pay more if you are overweight, smoke, or have ongoing medical issues. The younger and healthier you are, the less you will pay.

Take note that the proceeds of your life insurance will go to whoever is designated as the beneficiary, even if that is a different person than who is specified in your will. You need to keep this up to date, especially when your circumstances change. If you want the insurance to go to a minor, it needs to be left to a trustee or guardian for the minor, rather than directly to the child, to avoid major headaches in collecting the money.

How much is enough? This can be a difficult question to answer. But you can break it down by considering what you want the insurance to cover:

- How much of your income would you like to replace for your survivors and for how long? Since insurance money isn't subject to income tax, you can base this on your after-tax contribution to the family budget.

- How much would the family need to pay for health insurance?

- If you are divorced, do you need to replace what you owe in child support? Or, conversely, would your family need to pay someone to do the housework or child care that you now do?

- Are you committed to paying for all or part of the cost to send the children to private school or college?

- Do you want your spouse or partner to be able to pay off the mortgage or other debts or be able to add to a retirement fund?

- Are there other special needs—such as funds for siblings or charitable contributions—that also need to be covered?

Buying life insurance for this whole list could add up to a large amount—more than you can really afford. If so, make sure you have at least insurance equal to a few years of your income if you have a family that relies on you. Given the setbacks you've already dealt with, almost nothing would be worse for your family than being left without any financial resources at all.

DISABILITY INSURANCE

Disability insurance provides all or a portion of your income if you are too sick or disabled to work, either for a short time or for an extended period. Many employers offer some disability coverage as part of the benefits package, though you sometimes have to pay for it through a payroll deduction.

If you are a single parent or a significant wage earner in

your household or if you provide child support, you should give serious consideration to this kind of insurance, so that you and your family aren't in a financial bind if you can't work. The Council on Disability Awareness, a nonprofit supported by disability insurers, says that one-third of Americans entering the workforce today will have some kind of illness or injury in their lifetime that prevents them from working for a time. The average long-term disability, commonly from back injuries, cancer, heart disease, or other illnesses, is about two and a half years.

If you are disabled, you may qualify for disability payments under Social Security. However, these can be difficult to qualify for, they can take months to kick in, and they may not replace very much of your income. You may also be able to tap your IRA without penalty if you are disabled. You still have to pay income tax on any withdrawals—and that money won't be there if you recover and need income in retirement.

Short-term disability insurance will cover the bulk of your paycheck for a few months. Long-term disability usually replaces about 60 percent of your income for some period of time.

To understand what kind of coverage you have, here are some questions to ask or details to look for:

- How long must I be disabled before the benefits kick in? Long-term benefits can kick in as soon as thirty days after a disability or as much as six months later.

- What percentage of my pay will be replaced? Are bonuses or commissions included?

- Will the payment go up as my income increases or will there be cost-of-living increases?

- Are preexisting conditions, like cancer, back problems, or depression, excluded? If so, for how long? Are any other kinds of illnesses or injuries excluded?

- Will the insurance cover me if I can't work in my current occupation? Or does it apply only if I can't do any job?

- How long will the payments last? Some policies limit disability payments to two or five years, whereas others continue if you are disabled until you reach sixty-five years of age.

If you are self-employed, you may be able to buy a policy through an insurance agent, at a cost of up to 4 percent of your gross annual pay. But the insurer will base its payouts on your net pay, after your business expenses, and may add other exclusions. Expensive as it is, if you are the sole earner for a family, it's worth consideration.

OTHER INSURANCE PRODUCTS

Through television ads, marketing calls, mail promotions, and credit card inserts, you may feel bombarded with offers of different kinds of insurance: "mortgage insurance" to pay your mortgage or "debt protection" to cover your credit card if you can't; cancer insurance; insurance that pays a little every day when you're sick.

Generally, none of that is worth the cost. Helpful insurance is broad, covering a range of illnesses or disabilities or costs. Your likelihood of needing a very specific insurance, like insurance to pay your debts if you can't, is very small—and the coverage is fairly expensive for what you get.

You'll be much better off if you build up a cash account with up to six months of living expenses. Then you'll have money to pay for the small things that happen to your car or house, and you'll have funds for any emergency that occurs.

CHAPTER 9

MANAGING YOUR MONEY FOR THE LONG TERM

Saving and investing are a challenge in the best of times, but they're especially trying when you're starting over. If you've divorced, you may have seen the cost of lawyers and the process of dividing up assets chew up all your best efforts at savings and retirement investments, setting you back. If you've lost a spouse, you may feel like you're adrift, without any guidance on where to go next. And if you've lost a job or been through a financial crisis, you may well be starting your long-term investing from scratch—if you ever actually started it at all.

None of this is easy. Investing your money for retirement, education, and other long-term needs can feel abstract and confusing. If you haven't handled your own investments before, you'll discover that money management comes with a whole new vocabulary and some complex concepts. But despite the many difficulties of investing, it's the most promising method you have to help your money grow into a genuine nest egg. In addition, a strong investment portfolio can help protect you from future financial disruptions by giving you a cushion to fall back on.

To get that result, you don't need to be a math whiz or a fortune-teller or an expert at reading stock charts. Instead, you just need to develop enough of an understanding and comfort level with the concepts that you can make smart decisions on your own or sign off with confidence on what an adviser recommends. The following is intended to be a primer to get you going in that direction, particularly if you are feeling insecure about your ability to invest or you haven't done this on your own before.

THE BIG CONCEPTS OF SUCCESSFUL INVESTING

Just as good nutrition comes with some basic guidelines, successful investing also comes with some basic rules of thumb.

The more you save, the better you'll do.

Unless you were born into wealth, you probably will have to provide a substantial amount of money toward your retirement. Social Security will cover only so much, and pensions are growing rare. Will you have enough? The answer to that question will ride largely on how much you save over your lifetime.

Admittedly, this sounds pretty obvious. But it's also a very big idea. Many people spend a lot of time and energy deciding which stocks to buy or sell or exactly which mutual funds to put in a portfolio. But none of that will matter if your savings are puny.

Say you invest in a stock that does very well, increasing tenfold over a period of time, which happens occasionally with great stocks. If you invested $1,000 in such a stock, your investment would grow to $10,000 or maybe more—impressive returns, but not enough to pay for a semester of college these days. But say you started with $10,000. A tenfold return would give you $100,000, enough perhaps to pay for a bachelor's degree at most state universities, with some money left over.

If you are disciplined and aim to put away 10 percent or

more of your income every year, you will probably be very comfortable in retirement. (In addition, you will already know how to live within a specific budget, which also will pay off during retirement.) You may not be able to do that every year, especially if you have been out of work, changed careers, or faced financial setbacks. But it's a worthy goal and one worth working up to.

If you put off saving, or never save more than 2 percent or 3 percent of what you bring in every year—or worse, repeatedly spend what you have saved—you could easily face the prospect that you will need to keep working much longer than you expected and that you could run out of money in your old age. If you're terrible at putting away money, try to keep in mind the bigger picture: you are saving for your own very special future.

The easiest way to pay yourself first is to contribute to a work retirement plan or set up a savings account or mutual fund that automatically debits your bank account after every paycheck is deposited. You can also put away money monthly or make one big contribution from an annual bonus. Some people put all their rebates and coupon savings into a savings account for vacations, or make a point of saving a little bit (or all) of every windfall, whether it's a tax refund or an unexpected inheritance. However you do it, saving early, often, and generously will give you many more options in the future.

Different forms of savings—short-term, medium-term, and long-term—call for different approaches. Short-term savings should be in cash and should be easily accessible, whether in a regular or online savings account or a bank money market account or a money market mutual fund. Medium-term savings, which may be for a new home, vacations, cars, weddings, college, and as a deeper safety cushion, and long-term savings, primarily for retirement, can be invested in a mix of stocks and bonds.

A portfolio should be well diversified.

This is another big concept that is often misunderstood. A

diversified portfolio is very much like a balanced diet. It doesn't include one of everything from the buffet table, though it's easy (and tempting) to load up your plate like that. It isn't a diet made up entirely of broccoli—or ice cream. Instead, it reflects a mix of stocks, which represent ownership in companies and their profits, and bonds, or debt that companies and governments issue to fund their operations.

A diversified portfolio can be as simple as a 50-50 mix of a broad stock-market mutual fund and a broad bond-market mutual fund, or it could include a mix of domestic and international stocks and bonds, and investments in smallish, midsize, and very large companies. Owning more than eight or ten mutual funds is probably overkill. On the other hand, you probably need to own ten or more individual stocks to diversify your portfolio enough to reduce your overall risk.

What kind of a stock and bond mix will suffice for you depends on how far you are from needing the money and how much stomach you have for risk. While bonds can certainly fall in value, stocks are much more volatile as a group, with the potential to rise or fall as much as 40 percent or 50 percent in one year. The more years you have until your goal, the more risk you can take without suffering severe consequences; the closer your goal gets, the more you should move toward conservative investments to preserve the gains you have.

But you also need to weigh how well you can stand to lose money. If watching your portfolio shed 20 percent of its value makes you want to pull out your money and hide it in your bedroom closet, then take a more conservative approach.

In other words, a thirty-year-old who is thirty-five years from retirement could have 80 percent or 90 percent of a retirement portfolio in stocks. But if that person can't bear watching the value of the portfolio slide, then maybe stocks shouldn't be more than 60 or 70 percent of the mix. By contrast, a fifty-five-year-old with a high tolerance for risk might be okay with 60 or 70 percent of a retirement fund in stocks, while one with a low tolerance for risk might accept only 40 to

50 percent in stocks—enough to benefit from gains but not to lose what has been accumulated as retirement approaches.

For the most part, your end result won't change much if you have slightly more of your investments in stocks or bonds. It's having a mix that makes a difference.

Investing is a long-term sport.

If your goal is a quick return to recover a recent loss or to make up for lost time, go to the horse track. Because stocks and bonds can bounce around in value, you need to be patient over several years—not just days or months. Over time, your stock investments should grow faster than other kinds of investments and at a rate greater than inflation. But it isn't guaranteed, and in any given few-year period, you may lose money. That's why you need to tune out all the daily chatter about individual stocks and keep your eye on your original goal, whether it's retirement or paying for college or creating a financial cushion.

Successful investors learn not to obsess over every up and down in the market but to take the long view. Sure, they can take advantage of downturns by investing more and perhaps lightening up on some winners during boom times. (Remember, your goal is to buy low and sell high, though many people do the opposite, rushing in to buy when stocks are booming and running screaming from the room when they plunge.) But for the most part, slow and steady wins this race by helping you build college funds, retirement funds, or whatever other special funds you want to create over a period of time.

This is another reason why you should keep money that you will need in the next three to four years in safer investments, like savings accounts or money market accounts. If you are saving to buy a car or make a home down payment, you don't want to lose a dime of those dollars. For money you will need in the medium term, you might be more conservative as well, seeking investments that offer safer returns than a heavy mix of stocks.

Costs and expenses can make a huge difference in your long-term results.

Are you a careful shopper? A coupon clipper? Do you notice when your favorite soft drink is on sale and stock up? If you are eager to give some oomph to your new financial situation, you can do that by paying close attention to what you pay in commissions, fees, and other expenses. Those costs matter long term because they compound. Every dollar that you lose to expenses today will translate into several dollars that you won't have in retirement.

Of course, all investing has some cost; your goal is to keep it down as much as possible. That means parsing out exactly how much you are paying in fees. A $15 commission or annual fee may seem modest, unless it also equals more than one percentage point of your investment. In the investment world, such fees are often described in *basis points*, with 100 basis points equaling one percentage point or, turned around, 1 basis point equaling one-hundredth of a percentage point. Some very inexpensive mutual funds charge as little as 10 or 12 basis points in expenses annually, or $10 for a $10,000 investment. Some very expensive ones may have fees as high as 200 basis points. Sites like Morningstar.com rate and rank mutual funds on their expenses, and most mutual fund websites disclose the expense ratio in the fund's description.

You may be paying an adviser from 75 to 150 basis points to manage your money. But if he or she also then turns around and buys investments with high fees, you are giving up a significant part of your money to expenses—and that adviser may well be doing better than you are.

As a result, you should always ask exactly how much you'll be paying in expenses, commissions, and other fees, and question whether there are cheaper alternatives that are just as good.

THE BASIC FOOD GROUPS

Going back to the idea of a healthy diet, you want a mix of investments that will promote growth while reducing your risk of large losses. But first you need to know what's in the components. If you feel like you've never quite understood what all those investing pieces are, here's a rundown.

STOCKS

As mentioned earlier, stocks or *equities* represent a small ownership in a company. As a part owner, a stockholder should benefit over time when a company's profits climb—and lose when the profits plummet. On any given day, however, a stock may go up or down based on disclosures by the company, news about the industry or the broader economy, or world events.

Stockholders vote for the board of directors and may receive dividends, or a portion of profits, which are usually paid quarterly.

In the world of electronic trading that we live in today, you can buy or sell a stock just about any hour of the day. But generally, the trading day in the United States is from 9:30 A.M. to 4:00 P.M. Eastern time. During that time, the price of a given stock may change every second, going up or down by pennies or dollars as buyers and sellers trade shares.

When you hear talk about "the stock market," people usually are referring to the Dow Jones Industrial Average, an index of thirty large US stocks that is considered to represent the overall market trends. Sometimes the Dow rises or falls because many of the stocks in the index are rising or falling; sometimes one stock can account for most of the movement, and sometimes the economy or other world events—rather than the companies themselves—drive the index up or down.

The Dow is just one narrow index of the US market. The Standard & Poor's 500 Index combines five hundred large-company stocks, generally those with a market value of $10 billion or more. Funds that mirror that index are a popular investment. The Russell 2000 is an index of small-company stocks, which, for the most part, have a market value of up to about $2 billion. (Companies with market values between

$2 billion and $10 billion are considered "mid-caps.") The Wilshire 5000 Index and the MSCI US Broad Market Index both try to capture the movement of the whole US stock market at once.

To track a stock, it helps to know its "ticker" symbol, a two- to four-letter shorthand designation. When you look up a stock price, you'll get a whole table full of numbers: the current price, the high and low prices for the day, the volume (or how many shares traded that day), the high and low price for the last year, and the market capitalization, or the total dollar value the stock market places on that company.

The charts also include a *price-to-earnings ratio*, which shows the company's stock price divided by its annual earnings per share. This measure shows how much the market values the stock by depicting how much investors will pay for each $1 of earnings. Generally, the higher the P/E ratio, the more the stock market values that company. In stable times, the P/E ratio allows investors to compare stocks within and across industries and to weigh whether they think a stock is overvalued or undervalued. During the financial crisis, however, stocks were in such disfavor that many people didn't want to own them at any price and the traditional methods of assessing and valuing stocks temporarily lost their meaning.

When you buy or sell a stock, you'll pay a commission to a brokerage firm for executing the trade. The price can be as little $7 or $8 if you trade online using a discount brokerage firm and more than $75 if you work with a stockbroker at a full-service brokerage firm.

Stocks never expire or mature. But some companies will buy back their stock to reduce the number of shares outstanding and make up for new shares that are issued, such as stock options (or the right to buy shares in the future at a set price) that are granted to executives and employees as part of their compensation.

Stocks come in all kinds of flavors. Some are slow and steady, like shares of regulated utilities, which don't grow

READING A STOCK QUOTE

Apple Inc.
NASDAQ: AAPL

(1) Market open

$357.52

(2) Change   +0.32 +0.09%

Volume   13.71m

(3) Jul 8, 2011 2:37 p.m.

Quotes are delayed by 20 min

Previous close	**$ 357.20**

Day low	Day high
$352.20	**$359.89**

Open: 353.34

52 week low	52 week high
$235.56	**$364.90**

(4)	Market cap	**$325.29B**
	Average volume	**13.96M**
(5)	P/E ratio	**17.12**
	EPS	**20.89**
(6)	Dividend	**N/A**
	Div yield	**N/A**
	Ex dividend date	**11/21/95**

1. The closing (or current) price
2. The change from the previous closing price
3. How many shares traded today
4. The stock market value today, calculated by multiplying the stock price by the shares outstanding
5. The price-to-earnings ratio, the stock price divided by the earnings per share over the last four quarters
6. Apple's earnings per share over the most recent four quarters

---

very fast, but are generally predictable and pay decent cash dividends. Others, often called *growth stocks*, are known for their potential to soar; investors treasure them for their ability to record rapidly increasing profits every year and they tend to have high P/E ratios. At various times, Wal-Mart, Starbucks, Apple, and Amazon.com have been impressive growth stocks. Others are *value stocks*, companies that the market has underestimated and that investors think should be more highly valued than they are. The famous investor Warren Buffett is most noted for identifying underachieving value stocks and riding them to new heights. Value stocks tend to trade at a low P/E ratio—though it can be hard to tell whether a company is truly troubled or has just hit a rough spot in the road.

Investing in individual stocks can be profitable, but only if you are committed to spending time researching, studying, and staying on top of your stock selections. Because individuals don't have the tools, the access to company executives, or the time to track stocks closely, most small investors are at a disadvantage to the pros. As recently as a decade ago, many stockbrokers and financial advisers would recommend individual stocks to their clients, but today they are more likely to focus most of their recommendations on mutual funds and exchange-traded funds (see below) or turn over the bulk of the investing to professional money managers, who spend all their time studying the market.

If you want to learn more about stock investing, you can set aside a small percentage of your investments to try your hand at it or join an investment club, where a group of people meet monthly to create and follow a portfolio. There are also shelves of books about investing. A few classics include *The Intelligent Investor* by Benjamin Graham, *Common Stocks and Uncommon Profits and Other Writings* by Philip A. Fisher, *Stocks for the Long Run* by Jeremy Siegel, and *The Five Rules for Successful Stock Investing* by Pat Dorsey.

Preferred stock. Preferred stocks are less volatile than common stocks because they pay a regular, preset quarterly dividend, reflecting less on the company's growth and more on its ability to pay that dividend. Dividends on preferred stocks must be paid before common dividends, and a company in financial trouble must pay preferred shareholders before they pay common stockholders. Because they are more stable, somewhat like bonds, preferred stocks will show up in mutual funds that seek dividend returns or to reduce the risk of common-stock investing.

Convertible preferred stocks. These stocks come with an option to be converted to common stock at a specific conversion rate. Start-up companies often issue preferred stock to early investors, which is converted to common stock when the company has its initial public offering or sells its first common shares to the public.

BONDS

Bonds are a kind of long-term debt issued by companies and governments to investors to help fund their operations. Most bonds are sold in increments of $1,000. While stocks are described by their ticker symbol, bonds are described by the interest rate they pay, also known as the coupon, and the year the debt matures or comes due. Because they pay interest regularly, usually twice a year, they are also known as *fixed-income* investments.

Between the time they are issued and when they mature, bonds may be traded between investors, with prices rising and falling based on interest rates in the broader economy and how risky the debt is believed to be. Bond prices and interest rates in the marketplace move in opposite directions, with prices rising when interest rates fall and prices falling as interest rates rise.

The *yield to maturity* is the annual return an investor expects to get if a bond is held until it matures. Some bonds can be repaid earlier than their maturity date; that earlier date is known as the *call date*. The *yield to call* is the annual return an investor expects to get if the bond is redeemed on the call date.

Generally speaking, bonds are considered safer than stocks. If a company runs into financial trouble, it will pay interest on its debt before it pays dividends to shareholders, and bondholders will be repaid before shareholders receive anything.

However, if you need cash and want to sell a bond before

it matures, you could get more or less than its $1,000 face value, depending on interest rates and other factors. In addition, because some bonds don't trade very often, individual bonds may be more difficult to sell than stocks and you may not always get the best price for them. The selection of bonds to buy may be limited and because brokerage firms often sell what is in their inventory, it can be hard to know if the price that is offered is fair. You can buy Treasurys direct from the government at www.TreasuryDirect.gov.

Bonds typically are rated by bond-rating firms like Standard & Poor's and Moody's Investors Service, with a gradelike system describing how likely (or unlikely) they are to be paid in full. For years, investors looked to those ratings as a reliable guide about how much risk they were taking on. But in the financial crisis of 2008–09, many highly rated bonds in the financial-services industry lost substantial value, and several major financial firms with investment-grade ratings were unable to meet their obligations. The debacle both tarnished the reputation of the ratings agencies and provided a harsh reminder that bonds can be quite risky, too.

Standard & Poor's	Moody's	Meaning
AAA	Aaa	Highest quality, minimal risk
AA	Aa	High quality, low credit risk
A	A	Upper medium grade, low credit risk
BBB	Baa	Medium grade
BB	Ba	Substantial credit risk, "junk bonds"
B	B	Speculative
CCC	Caa	High credit risk
CC	Ca	High credit risk, likely near default
D	C	Typically in default

READING BOND PRICES

Issuer Name	Symbol	① Coupon	② Maturity	③ Rating Moody's/S&P/ Fitch	④ High	Low	Last	Change
BANK OF AMERICA CORP	BAC.ABP	3.625%	Mar 2016	A2/A/A+	101.613	99.839	100.189	-0.560
GENERAL ELECTRIC CAPITAL CORP	GE.HPG	1.875%	Sep 2013	Aa2/AA+/--	101.854	100.920	100.941	-0.293
WAL-MART STORES	WMT.AB	5.625%	Apr 2041	Aa2/AA/AA	104.877	103.505	104.877	0.599
BANK OF AMERICA CORP	BAC.ACQ	5.000%	May 2021	A2/A/A+	101.132	98.703	99.555	-0.445
PETROBRAS INTL FINANCE CO	PBR.AB	5.375%	Jan 2021	A3/BBB-/BBB	104.179	103.153	103.591	-0.049
JPMORGAN CHASE & CO	JPM.SCH	3.150%	Jul 2016	--/A+/--	101.500	100.243	100.440	-0.299
CENTURYLINK	CTL.HE	6.450%	Jun 2021	Baa3/BB/BBB-	103.301	100.805	103.293	2.082
MORGAN STANLEY	MS.PI	5.300%	Mar 2013	A2/A/A	105.837	105.421	105.837	-0.624
HEWLETT-PACKARD CO	HPQ.AD	4.300%	Jun 2021	A2/A/A+	102.567	101.559	102.425	0.146

1. The interest rate paid annually
2. When the bond is to be repaid
3. Bond rating, assessing its riskiness

4. Prices shortened. A bond priced at 100.189 would actually be $1,001.89

Corporate bonds are issued by companies, and the interest they pay is taxable. Municipal bonds are issued by cities and states and usually are exempt from federal income tax and income taxes in the state that issued them. Municipal bonds usually pay a lower interest rate to reflect the tax break that comes with them, so they are most valuable to people who are in high tax brackets. Treasurys are debt issued to fund the federal government, with Treasury bills maturing within a year, Treasury notes maturing within ten years, and Treasury bonds maturing in more than ten years.

Because interest rates move up and down with the economy and other factors, people who want safe, regular income often will build a bond *ladder*. To do that, the investor may buy bonds that mature in two years, four years, six years, and eight years. As each bond matures, it is replaced with a bond that matures in eight years. Bonds that mature several years in the future often pay higher interest rates than short-term debt, but they are also more likely to fluctuate in price, so a ladder increases the overall interest while reducing the risk involved.

MUTUAL FUNDS

By pooling funds from lots of investors, mutual funds give small fry the chance to invest in a much broader portfolio of investments that would be otherwise impossible to put together on their own. Because funds come in an almost endless variety of combinations, many investors use them for all their investing. And if you have a 401(k) or 403(b) through your job, you probably have your retirement funds in mutual funds as well.

Mutual funds are just about the simplest ways to invest because you can choose from a number of all-purpose funds, add your money, and simply check on your investments every month or every quarter.

For the most part, you want to focus on two kinds of mutual funds: *no-load funds,* which don't have sales charges when you buy or sell; and *index funds,* which are based on indexes like the S&P 500 Index of large-company stocks, the Wilshire 5000 Index of the total market, or the Russell 2000 Index of small-cap stocks.

Why these? One of your main goals in investing is to keep your expenses down. If you pay a load, or sales charge, you start out at a loss because some amount of your investment was spent before you started. Index funds usually are among the cheapest funds around because the people who run them only have to mimic a market index rather than researching and picking stocks and bonds. Managed funds, by contrast, have higher expenses because highly paid professionals select and monitor every investment. In addition, most managed funds don't do as well as index funds over time.

Beware, however, that some index funds come with unusually high costs. If you aren't sure if the one you've picked or an adviser is recommending is a good one, go to Morning star.com or LipperLeaders.com to compare your fund's expenses and performance with others in the same category.

Mutual fund expenses can be sort of mystifying. While you see the commission you pay when you buy a stock by itself, a no-load mutual fund's expenses are part of the fund's operating cost, so the return you get is after the expenses have been paid. To see how large the fund's ongoing expenses are, you

UNDERSTANDING MUTUAL FUND PRICES

VANGUARD INDEX FUNDS: VANGUARD 500 INDEX FUND; INVESTOR SHARES   VFINX

1 As of 7/7/11
NAV: 124.72

2 1-Day Net Change
▲ 1.30

1-Day Return
▲ 1.05%

3 YTD Total Return
▲ 8.63%

4 Category
S&P 500 Index

LIPPER LEADER SCORECARD

5 ⑤ ⑤ ⑤ ⑤ ⑤

Total Return   Consistent   Preservation   Tax   Expense
                   Return   Efficiency

Higher ⑤ ④ ③ ② ① Lower

More on Lipper Leaders

TOTAL RETURNS (%) 3, 5 and 10 year returns are annualized.

6	YTD	1Yr	3Yr	5Yr	10Yr
Fund	8.63	30.00	4.89	3.44	3.16
Category	8.39	29.43	4.42	2.98	2.74
Index (S&P 500)	8.70	30.20	5.00	3.50	3.30
% Rank in Category	19	16	16	12	11
Quintile Rank	A	A	A	A	A

FUND STATS

Portfolio Style:	S&P 500 Index
7 Net Assets ($Mil):	30,461.60
Inception Date:	8/31/76
8 Expense Ratio:	0.17%
Sales Charge:	
Load Type	No Load
9 Front-End Load	0.00%
Back-End Load	0.00%

Investment Policy: The Fund seeks capital appreciation. Fidelity Management & Research normally invests at least 65% of assets in common stock of firms that they believe have the potential for dividend growth by either increasing their dividends or commencing dividends, if none are currently paid.

TOP 10 HOLDINGS (as of 3/31/11) **10**

Name	% Net Assets
Exxon Mobil Ord	3.46
Apple Inc Ord	2.67
Chevron Corp Ord	1.79
General Electric Ord	1.77
Int Bus Ord	1.65
Microsoft Corp Ord	1.56
Jpmorgan Chase & Co Ord	1.52
At&t Inc Ord	1.50
Procter & Gamble Co Ord	1.43
Wells Fargo & Co Ord	1.39

11 PURCHASE INFO

Status to New Investors:	Open
Manager Name:	Michael H. Buek
Manager Start Date:	2001
Initial Purchase Regular:	$3,000
Phone Number:	800-662-7447

DISTRIBUTION HISTORY

Year	Income Distribution	Capital Gains Distribution
YTD	$ 0.51	NA
2010	$ 1.97	NA
2009	$ 2.10	NA
2008	$ 2.51	NA

1. NAV or net asset value, the price an investor pays
2. The price change since the previous trading date
3. Performance year-to-date
4. Fund category
5. How Lipper rates the fund
6. How the fund has performed over time
7. Net assets reflect how much money is invested in the fund, in millions
8. The expenses investors pay
9. Additional fees or "loads" that investors would pay
10. Top stocks held
11. Manager information and minimum initial purchase

may need to go to the mutual fund website or Morningstar .com and look them up. The lowest expenses on index funds are around 10 basis points, or about $10 a year for every $10,000 invested. Many managed funds, however, have expenses well above 1 percent, or more than $100 for every $10,000 invested.

Mutual funds are priced based on their net asset value, the value of the investments divided by the number of shares outstanding. The net asset value will fluctuate along with the investments, but generally, you'll only see one price a day, based on the prices after the most recent trading day has ended.

Many mutual funds require a minimum initial investment of at least $2,000 or as much as $10,000, which can be a high bar for a new investor. If you're just starting out, look for funds that waive that initial minimum if you invest $50 or $100 every month directly from your checking account. You'll get in the habit of saving and investing regularly, and you'll be buying both when the market is high and when it is low, which is known as *dollar-cost averaging*. When you invest in that disciplined way, you don't have to worry about whether you're buying when the market is overheated because your purchases will average out over time.

Among the thousands of funds are just about every combination possible. You can buy funds of large-cap, mid-cap, and small-cap stocks, growth stocks and value stocks, domestic stocks, international stocks, and emerging-market stocks. Taxable and tax-free money market mutual funds offer relatively safe options for your cash, though they aren't federally insured like bank money market accounts.

Bond funds are a bit more complicated. Because they hold many bonds, you have a more broadly diversified portfolio than you could create on your own. But when interest rates are falling, bond funds price can climb—and when interest rates are rising quickly, bond fund prices can fall sharply, leaving you with a surprising loss for an investment with a reputation for being stable. Because an individual bond will eventually mature, you can ignore those swings in price if you intend to hold the bond to maturity. But bond mutual funds never mature because managers are always buying and selling bonds.

Short-term bond funds tend to be less volatile because the bonds are close to maturity. But they also usually pay lower interest rates than longer-term bonds. By contrast, long-term bond funds may pay higher rates, but may also fluctuate far more in price. That's why many experts recommend you buy a medium-term bond fund, which should pay higher interest than short-term bonds but be less volatile than long-term bonds.

In addition to different maturities, you can also choose mutual funds with government or corporate bonds, mortgage bonds like Ginnie Maes, and high-yield bonds (also known as junk bonds), which carry higher interest rates because the companies that issue them are considered riskier than average.

Balanced funds offer a combination of stocks and bonds and are intended to temper the riskiness of stocks with the stability of bonds, smoothing out returns. Included in that category are *target date* or *life-cycle* funds, which are designed to invest more heavily in stocks when you're far from your retirement goal and move into more conservative investments as you move toward your senior years. If you choose that option, pick the fund with the year closest to your expected retirement.

With so many choices and possible combinations, how do you pick what to do? Many people go overboard, trying to put every kind of option on the buffet into a portfolio. But there's an easier way. The MarketWatch website tracks eight "lazy portfolios," made up of three to eleven different mutual funds, and all of them have generally outperformed the S&P 500 Index over time. Investment adviser Allan Roth's Second Grader's Starter portfolio, for instance, invests like this:

- 60 percent in the Vanguard Total Stock Market Fund

- 30 percent in the Vanguard Total International Stock Fund

- 10 percent in the Vanguard Total Bond Market Fund

Financial author William Bernstein's No Brainer portfolio allocates 25 percent each to the following:

- Vanguard 500 Index Investor

- Vanguard European Stock Fund

- Vanguard Small Cap Fund

- Vanguard Total Bond Market Fund

And the Margaritaville portfolio from financial columnist Scott Burns puts one-third each in the following:

- Vanguard Total Stock Market Fund

- Vanguard Total International Stock Fund

- Vanguard Inflation Protected Securities Fund

Each of the preceding portfolios would be easy to replicate, as are the other options.

Once you've made the investment, all you have to do is rebalance once or twice a year. That is, you check on your portfolio and move money around to get back to the same ratios that you started with. You may not have a big windfall to brag about at your kids' soccer games, but in the long run, you'll probably do better than many Wall Street professionals and you will sleep well, too.

Exchange-Traded Funds

Exchange-traded funds (ETFs) are the newest arrows in the investment quiver, and although they seem complicated, they really aren't. Essentially, they act like mutual funds, mimicking a stock or bond index or specializing in a sector, like clean energy or technology. But because of the way they're designed, they generate fewer tax liabilities, and they often have lower expenses than mutual funds.

UNDERSTANDING
EXCHANGE TRADED FUND PRICES

ETF SNAPSHOT Sign up for Price & Volume Alerts

(1) **Vanguard T StMk Idx;ETF (VTI)** (2) (3)
4:00 pm ET 7/8/11
Price: **$69.76** Change: **-0.50** % Change: **-0.71%** Volume: **1,598,020** 52 Week High: **71.11** 52 Week Low: **52.98**

Performance (%) total return, cumulative through prior close.

	VTI	SP500
1 Day	1.08	1.04
1 Week	2.72	2.52
4 Weeks	5.55	5.12
13 Weeks	2.06	1.83
1 Year	32.66	29.43
3 Years	19.90	13.86
5 Years	23.57	15.63

(4)

VTI Daily — 7/08/11

Compare to Index: Select
Period: 1D | 1W | 4W | 13W | 1Y | 3Y | 5Y Custom ▶
▶ Go to Interactive Charting

Note: Comparisons show price change only; not total return.

(5)

Investment Information

Market Cap	$20,686,511,280
Net Assets	$20,102,600,000
NAV	$70.25
Prem/Discount	0.01%
Shares Outstanding	294,428,000
Avg Daily Vol	1,893,800
Dividend Yield %	1.61
Latest Dividend	$0.28 - 06/24/2011

The Fund seeks to track the performance of a benchmark index that measures the investment return of the overall stock market. The Fund employs a "passive management" approach designed to track the performance of the MSCI US Broad Market Index.

Dividend yield is based on regular and irregular dividends and may not reflect an established regular annual rate. Initial monthly and quarterly dividends are annualized and presented as an annual yield.

Detailed Information

Style	Core
Market Cap Classification	Multi-Cap
Asset Class	Equity
Inception Date	05/24/2001
Primary Exchange	NYSE ARCA
Mgmt Co	Vanguard Group Inc
Administrator	Vanguard Group Inc
Turnover	5.00
Beta	1.04
P/E	20.65
P/B	3.75
Expense Ratio *	0.06

* expense ratio updated annually from fund's year-end report

(6)

Top 10 Holdings (7)

Company Name	% of Total Portfolio	Dollar Value (in thousands)
EXXON MOBIL CORP ORD	2.82%	$566,893.32
APPLE INC ORD	2.13%	$428,185.38
CHEVRON CORP ORD	1.44%	$289,477.44
GENERAL ELECTRIC COMPANY ORD	1.42%	$285,456.92
INTERNATIONAL BUSINESS MACHINES CORP ORD	1.35%	$271,385.10
MICROSOFT CORP ORD	1.30%	$261,333.80
AT AND T INC ORD	1.20%	$241,231.20
JPMORGAN CHASE & CO ORD	1.20%	$241,231.20
PROCTER & GAMBLE CO ORD	1.15%	$231,179.90
JOHNSON & JOHNSON ORD	1.08%	$217,108.08
Total:	15.09%	$3,033,482.34

Sector Allocations **Historical Quotes**

1. The current price
2. Change from the previous closing price
3. The number of shares traded today
4. Performance vs a benchmark, the S&P 500
5. General information
6. Expenses investors pay
7. Top stocks held in the fund

The biggest different between an ETF and a mutual fund is that an ETF is bought and sold like a stock and you can buy it at any time of the day, generally paying a commission when you buy and sell it. There is no minimum purchase, so you can buy $500 or $1,000 worth of an ETF if you want. If you're investing regularly every month or two, you'll prefer a mutual fund over an ETF because those commissions can add up. (Some firms have waived commissions on certain ETFs.) But if you are investing an annual bonus check or several months of savings, an ETF may be a cheaper alternative.

Like mutual funds, there are many types of ETFs, including some very complex funds designed primarily for professional investors. Because professionals may buy and sell daily, these funds aren't meant for the buy-and-hold investor. Instead, stick with the basic ETFs, like well-known stock and bond index funds.

TAX ISSUES

Investing has some tax advantages. If you hold many investments—stocks, bonds, mutual funds, or ETFs—for at least a year and sell them for a gain, that gain will be taxed at the capital gains rate, currently a maximum of 15 percent, which is lower than most income-tax rates. Likewise, most common and preferred dividends are taxed at a maximum of 15 percent. Interest on corporate bonds, savings accounts, and certificates of deposit, however, are taxed like your regular pay.

If you sell an investment at a loss, that loss can be used to offset your investment gains. If your losses are more than your gains, you can use up to $3,000 in losses a year to reduce your other income, cutting your tax bill. If you still have some investment losses left over, you can carry those losses forward and use them to reduce next year's tax bill.

You may also have to pay taxes on capital gains, dividends, and interest on investments in your mutual funds. At the end of each year, you'll receive a statement from your mutual fund company outlining how much the fund made in capital gains or paid out in dividends or interest. Because mutual fund managers are always buying and selling stocks, it's possible that you could pay capital gains taxes on a fund that lost money that year.

Both the capital gains rate and the dividend rate are set to increase in 2013, which could make stock investing, in particular, more expensive. There's always a chance, of course, that Congress could change its mind.

Many retirement investments and college savings plans offer special tax advantages, as we'll see in the next sections.

RETIREMENT FUNDS

No matter how old you are, you need to be thinking about retirement almost from the moment you begin working for pay. Even if you're a teacher or in another job where you will have a pension at retirement, you probably won't receive enough money after inflation to enjoy your current lifestyle without some additional funds. If you will have only Social Security, you will definitely need additional income to live comfortably. And unless you inherit that money, it's going to have to come from you.

It helps to begin saving for retirement early, but it's never too late to start—especially since your senior years are going to come whether you're prepared for them or not. Besides, there are strong incentives to put money in retirement accounts: many employers offer matching contributions, and the government offers tax advantages.

Still not convinced? Try calculating how much you will need in retirement based on your new situation, a number that may be quite sobering. Start with your current budget—how much you need now to pay your bills and stay comfortable. If you have kids at home, try to subtract the extra amounts you spend on them. If you think your home will be

paid off in retirement, you can subtract that mortgage payment, too. While you may not be as active in retirement as you
are now, you may have higher health-care costs. So your income needs then may not be that much lower than your personal needs now.

Say you'll need $40,000 a year to live on. Maybe your pen-
sion will provide most of that and you won't have to add in
much on your own. But without a pension, Social Security may
provide you only $15,000 a year. To get to $40,000 a year, you'll
need to come up with $25,000 a year for up to thirty years after
you retire, since none of us knows if we'll live to be seventy-five,
eighty-five, or ninety-five years old. To be sure you don't run
out of money, you'll need at least $500,000 to $600,000 in savings. If you retire before you get your full Social Security benefit, you'll need even more than that.

MAXIMIZING YOUR SOCIAL SECURITY BENEFITS

Most workers can begin receiving Social Security benefits at age 62, but they will be
discounted as much as 30 percent from the rate you could receive at full retirement.
Here's how old you need to be to receive the full amount:

If you were born	Age of full retirement
1943 to 1954	66 years old
1955	66 and 2 months
1956	66 and 4 months
1957	66 and 6 months
1958	66 and 8 months
1959	66 and 10 months
1960 and after	67 years old

To reach your goal, ideally, you will sock away about 10
percent of your pay toward retirement each year, and if you're
lucky, an employer will provide a match of 3 percent to 6 percent of your pay. If saving 10 percent of your pay seems wildly

unlikely in your current budget, start with something small—
5 percent or even 2 percent if that's all you can do. Then every
time you get a raise, go online and increase your contribution
to your account. Each year, increase your total contribution by
a percentage point or two, until you get to your goal. If you
stick with it, eventually you will get there.

The following are the various types of retirement savings
options:

EMPLOYER PLANS

If you work for a company of much size, you probably have access to a 401(k) retirement plan, so named for the part of the
tax code that allows you to make your contribution before
taxes. If you work for a public-education system or a nonprofit,
you may have a 403(b) instead. Despite the different names,
they work similarly.

When you are hired, you can designate what percentage
of your pay you want to contribute to the retirement plan and
you can change your contribution at any time. Under IRS
rules, you can contribute up to $16,500 in 2011, plus an addi-
tional $5,500 in "catch-up" contribution for those fifty and
older. Whatever amount you designate, it will be deducted
from your paycheck before income taxes, Social Security, or
Medicare taxes are applied, meaning the contribution will reduce your taxable income. That tax break means you'll also be
keeping a bigger portion of your paycheck, even if some of it
is socked away for later.

Many employers also offer a company match. Because you
never want to leave free money sitting on the table, you should
contribute enough to get your firm's full match. So if your
company matches half or all of your contribution up to 6 percent of your pay, you want to contribute at least 6 percent.
Failing to take advantage of the full match is like giving the
company back some of your paycheck.

At many companies, the company's match must *vest*,

meaning you may not receive the full company match until you have been in the plan one to six years. If you leave the company, you may lose the part of the match that hasn't yet vested. But that's no excuse for not doing your best to get it.

More and more, companies are automatically enrolling new employees in their 401(k) plans, even if you don't sign up. Some companies are even automatically increasing the contribution a little bit every year. That may feel heavy-handed, but it will help you out in the long run.

Once you sign up or if you are automatically enrolled, you'll also have to decide how you want your money invested. Your company probably will have a number of mutual fund choices and possibly some other kinds of investment choices as well. The list of choices should include information about how they have performed over the last year, three years, five years, and ten years and also what their expense ratios are. Hopefully, you'll have some good, low-cost index fund options and you can create one of those "lazy" portfolios above. Or depending on your age, you could put between 50 percent and 80 percent in an S&P 500 index fund or a total stock market fund and the rest in a total bond market fund, or an inflation-protected securities fund. (The younger you are, the more you can invest in stocks because you have a lot of years of savings ahead. The older you are, the more tempered you may want to be because you'll have fewer years to recover from downturns like 2008–09.)

If you feel like you have a lot of catching up to do to make up for your financial setback, you may be tempted to take more risk than you would otherwise by investing more heavily in stocks. That's okay if you're also prepared to watch your investments fall in value, sometimes sharply. If you are over forty, keep at least a small percentage of your retirement investments in bonds to provide some diversification.

If this all feels like a bunch of mumbo-jumbo to you, there is a very simple option called a *target-date* fund. These funds are designed to provide an appropriate mix of stocks and bonds, foreign and domestic investments, and other funds geared to how far you are from retirement. So if you are forty years old in 2012, then you want a 2035 or 2040 target-date fund. If you want to take a bit more risk for someone your age, then choose a fund a bit further out, like 2045. If you are risk averse, choose a fund that is a bit closer in, like 2030. Don't, however, split up your money among several target-date funds. They are meant to be a one-size-fits-all solution, and investing in different ones only muddies your results. Some people like to put some of their money in a target-date fund and then divide up some into their own mix of mutual funds. That's okay, but keep in mind that the target-date fund was created to do all the work for you.

These investments aren't perfect—though no investments are perfect. Some target-date funds got clobbered in the big stock-market decline because the funds that were part of the mix had more risk than expected. Sometimes these target-date funds have very high expenses, which reduce your overall return over time. A good target-date fund will have an expense ratio well below 1 percent and, hopefully, closer to the range of 70 to 75 basis points.

If your target-date fund's expense is a lot higher than that, you may want to invest some time and effort in making your own mutual fund choices. Research has found that cutting your expenses by 25 basis points over your career could have the same effect as getting an extra half-percentage point match from your employer.

If you were automatically enrolled, your company also chose your investment. Ideally, it was a target-date fund. If your money was put into a money market mutual fund or cash reserves account, consider transferring your investment to a target-date fund or a mix of stocks and bonds. While a money market fund is safe, it won't provide the returns over time that you will get from a better investment mix.

Many retirement-plan administrators offer tools, calculators, and model portfolios on their websites to help you sort through your choices. Phone representatives also offer support, but in most cases they are not fiduciaries, or those who are putting your best interests first. (See Chapter 2.) They may suggest investments that are more costly to you. So you'll have to be diligent in looking up or asking about your funds' expenses and performance and asking questions if there are terms or details you don't understand. That said, there are good reasons to seek out their counsel. People who get help with their retirement plans are more likely to have well-diversified accounts and to stay the course, even in a terrible financial crisis. That means they're still in when the market rebounds, while those who sold when the market was plunging can't benefit from its recovery.

A number of company retirement plans also offer professional advice, sometimes through services like Financial Engines, a company that specializes in providing retirement-plan advice. Sometimes these services charge as much as 60 basis points a year for this advice—or $60 for every $10,000 invested—which would reduce your returns in the long run. If you have more than $250,000 or $500,000 in your fund, the price goes down significantly. That advice is costly if you have a small account, but it may pay off for those who have a lot invested and worry about losing what they've worked so hard to build.

The other advantage of a 401(k) is that it grows tax-deferred, meaning you won't pay any taxes on your gains, interest, or dividends until you start to withdraw from it. Generally, you can begin taking money out after you turn fifty-nine and a half, though you might be able to start as early as fifty-five if you are laid off from your job. (Generally, you're better off leaving these funds in as long as possible. But if you need money to live in retirement, well, that's what you saved for.) When you make withdrawals in retirement, you'll pay taxes as though the money was regular income. But until then, it will have had a chance to grow without any deductions for the tax man.

Some companies offer two 401(k)s, a traditional version and a Roth 401(k). The main difference is in how they are treated for tax purposes. Contributions to the Roth version come out of your paycheck *after* you have paid all your taxes, rather than before. The contributions grow in the same way as with a traditional 401(k). But when the time comes to withdraw your money, you can do it tax-free, because you will have paid taxes on the front end.

Roth 401(k)s are most attractive to those who think their taxes will be much higher later in life than they are right now and who are willing to forgo a tax break now for one later. It's a tricky choice because some skeptics worry that many years from now Congress will change its mind and tax the gains on contributions to Roth accounts after all.

If that concerns you, or if you want a tax break now and some later, too, you can split your contributions up as long as you don't exceed the maximum contribution of $16,500, or $22,000 if you are over fifty years old.

INDIVIDUAL RETIREMENT ACCOUNTS

If you don't have a retirement plan through a workplace, you can to contribute to an IRA and maybe take a tax deduction, though the contribution levels are much less generous, and the rules can be complicated. In 2011, the maximum contribution per person was $5,000, plus another $1,000 if you are fifty or older, regardless of your income.

However, if you are married and don't work outside the home and your spouse has a retirement plan through work, you may deduct your IRA contribution only if your family adjusted gross income is less than $179,000.

As with 401(k)s, there are traditional IRAs and Roth IRAs. If you meet the income tests, you can deduct your contributions to traditional IRAs on your taxes. The contributions grow tax-deferred, and you pay taxes on the money as though it were a paycheck when you withdraw it in retirement. Roth contributions are made after tax and grow tax-free, so you aren't taxed again when you make retirement withdrawals. In addition, while there are penalties for early withdrawal of money in your traditional IRA, you can withdraw your Roth contributions at any time because you've already paid tax on them.

However, you can contribute to a Roth IRA only if your income is below certain limits. If you are a qualifying widow or file as married filing jointly, you can make a contribution if your 2011 adjusted gross income is less than $179,000. If you file as single or head of household, your 2011 adjusted gross income must be below $122,000.

Again, Roth IRAs make the most sense for people who believe their tax rate will be higher in retirement than it is now.

You can contribute to both a traditional IRA and a Roth IRA, but the total maximum contribution is the same—$5,000, or, if you are fifty or older, $6,000.

Note, however, that you can't contribute more to an IRA or Roth IRA than you earned. So if your total income was $3,000, you can contribute a maximum of $3,000 to an IRA or Roth IRA.

If you have a retirement plan at work, you may be able to supplement your savings with tax-deductible IRA contributions. If you are married filing jointly or a qualifying widow, your 2011 adjusted gross income can't be higher than $110,000, and if you are single or a head of household, your income must be under $66,000.

All these income limits are subject to change every year. If you aren't sure whether you can contribute or how much, check with the IRS or a financial adviser.

If you are self-employed, you may be able to contribute up to 25 percent of your income or up to $49,000 through a "simplified employee pension" or SEP-IRA.

TAKING OUT OR DIVIDING UP RETIREMENT MONEY

As you can tell by now, retirement accounts come with all kinds of rules and restrictions attached. If you aren't retirement age, almost any money you withdraw will be taxed as income plus an additional 10 percent penalty. Only a few exceptions allow you to avoid the penalty, such as if you are disabled or you need to pay for health insurance while you are unemployed.

Those rules make these accounts especially tricky if you inherit one or need to divide one up in a divorce. Even if you feel like the money in these funds is calling your name, don't touch it at least until you've talked to a professional. Here are some things to consider.

In a foreclosure or bankruptcy situation. Because saving for retirement is so important, the money in your 401(k) or IRA is protected from creditors in a bankruptcy, so you shouldn't withdraw those funds. After all, you will still need them later.

In addition, just about every way you can tap them comes with risks or extra costs. If you borrow from your 401(k), you will have to repay the money later, plus interest. If you can't repay it, you will have to pay taxes on it and additional penalties. You'll be better off doing everything in your power to keep those funds where they are.

If you lost a spouse. Assuming that you are the beneficiary of your spouse's IRA or 401(k)account, you most likely can roll the account over into your own IRA or 401(k) or into an account in your name and let the money grow tax-deferred to protect you in retirement or even provide for your heirs. Or, instead of that, you may be able to take out a little bit every year without penalty.

Before you do anything, however, check with the plan's administrator and with a financial adviser or lawyer to be sure you understand the various rules. The last thing you want to do is to pay extra taxes because you made a wrong move with a retirement account.

If you are divorcing. Sometimes retirement accounts must be split up as part of the dissolution of the marriage. To legally transfer money from one party to another, you'll need a *qualified domestic relations order,* or QDRO (sometimes pronounced Quad-row or Cue-dro). There are formal rules for executing the division of retirement money, and you'll need to check with the plan administrator to ensure that all the details are taken care of properly.

Keep in mind that this is pretax money, so you will owe tax on it whenever you take it out. Further, you won't be able to access these funds until retirement. It may make more sense to leave the retirement account with your ex so you have more cash now, some of which you can put away in an IRA or other savings, than to have funds that are out of reach for many years.

CHAPTER 10

Getting the Rest of Your Financial Life in Order

If you have made it this far, you have come a long way in restarting your financial life, gaining a lot of confidence along the way. You have made difficult decisions about your budget and where to live. You have taken steps to protect yourself and take care of your family's needs. And hopefully, you are saving and investing toward a brighter future.

There is just a bit more work to do—and unfortunately, it involves some of the more unpleasant aspects of adulthood: death and taxes. Even if you are moving on from a painful financial crisis or the death of spouse, you need to address this last bit of business, if for nothing else than to do the right thing for your children, siblings, and if they are still living, your parents. Admittedly, this isn't fun stuff. But the silver lining is that you can take care of it now and not have to think about it for a while.

TAXES

For the most part, paying income taxes is a universal experience and your new or evolving status by itself probably won't affect what has to be filed, when it must be filed, what kinds of forms you must fill out, or whether you have to pay taxes.

The following issues may be different, however.

If you are divorcing or divorced. If you are still married on December 31 of the tax year, then you can file as married, filing jointly, by the following April 15. If you are single, you may file as single, if you don't have any dependents, or you may qualify for the more favorable "head of household," if you have cared for a dependent and paid more than half the housing expenses.

Some exceptions exist, and state laws may vary on what constitutes married and unmarried, so if you aren't sure, ask a tax professional or call the IRS.

If you have lost a spouse. If your husband or wife died during the year, you can still file as married, filing jointly, for that year, including the income your spouse earned up until the date of death. (Income earned after that belongs to the estate, which may have to file its own tax return.)

If you have a dependent child, you can file as a *qualifying widow(er)* for two additional years if you haven't remarried, taking advantage of a higher standard deduction and more favorable tax rates.

If you have had debt cancelled because of financial setbacks. Generally, when a lender forgives all or part of a debt, such as the amount owed on a credit card or a personal loan, you have to pay income taxes on that amount. In those cases, the lender will report the amount to the IRS and send you a 1099-C. You will need to fill out Form 982 along with your regular Form 1040.

However, the Mortgage Forgiveness Debt Relief Act of 2007 makes an exception for up to $1 million of mortgage debt that is forgiven through a loan modification or a foreclosure, as long as the debt was for your principal residence. This tax break is in place through 2012. Even so, you still have to report the amount on Form 982.

In addition, debts discharged through bankruptcy proceedings aren't considered taxable income. And if you were insolvent when the debt was cancelled—that is, your liabilities exceeded your assets—you may not have to pay income taxes on some or all of the debt.

ADDRESSING YOUR OWN MORTALITY

This is unpleasant stuff, no doubt about it. But if you have experienced the death of a loved one before, you know that one of the nicest things you can do for your family and others who love you is to have informed them enough that they can help you out if you are ill and unable to speak for yourself or if you are dying.

These are some of the easiest decisions to put off—and yet some of the most crucial you will make. Taking care of them doesn't have to take a lot of time or be overly wrenching. And having just gone through a personal setback, all the issues that matter may still be fresh in your mind—all the more reason to just get this done. Here's your checklist.

Update or write your will. If you have a will, there's a good chance that it is out of date now. Your heirs or how you want your assets handled—or both—may have changed, and you may need to rethink that very important question of who will take care of your children if you die. If you put this off now, you may never get back to it.

If you don't have a will, you need one if you have any assets of value, such as a home, car, savings, or special collectibles. In addition, if you have children, you need to spell out who will care for them and who will look after their financial well-being and for how long. As part of a will, you will designate an executor, who will be responsible for dispersing your estate according to your wishes. You may also want to identify who will take care of your pets.

If you die *intestate*, or without a will, the state can decide who will get your assets and even who will raise your children. That's a risk that isn't worth taking.

If your will is very simple or if your budget is very tight, you can do your own through online services such as Nolo .com or LegalZoom.com. But the safest and most reliable approach is to hire a lawyer, who should ensure that you have properly taken care of the details according to your state laws. Especially if you have dependent children or a complex estate, it makes sense to hire a lawyer to draw up the will or at least to review the document you created online. In the back of your mind, remember that you may need to update it again as your life changes, your parents age, your children grow up, or you remarry.

Keep the will in a safe place, but not in a safe-deposit box, which can be hard to access immediately after someone's death.

Update or sign a power of attorney, health-care power of attorney, and living will. Again, the person you want to make these very important decisions for you may well have changed. A person with your power of attorney can step in for you and take care of your bills and your taxes and handle your money matters if you are unable to do so. This person can act on your behalf if you are out of the country or too ill to take care of your financial business. Choose someone who is good with finances and careful about making sure that things get done on time.

A health-care power of attorney and a living will spell out who can make medical decisions for you if you aren't able to do so and also detail your wishes if you are so ill or disabled that you aren't expected to recover. These are hard decisions, but they are immensely valuable to family members who otherwise must wrestle with whether to keep someone alive with a feeding tube or breathing tube regardless of the prognosis.

Some states require separate documents, while other states combine the two into one.

Even if you are young and very healthy, you need to make your wishes clear. Some of the biggest battles over end-of-life issues in recent years involved people who were unexpectedly incapacitated in their twenties.

The lawyer who draws up your will should also encourage you to sign such *advance directives*, as they are called. The additional cost of adding these documents should be very modest. However, if you want to do it on your own, CaringInfo.org has advance directives tailored to each state's laws, and Aging WithDignity.org charges $5 for a document called Five Wishes that describes your wishes in detail. The organization says the document is recognized in forty-two states.

Put a copy of these documents in your personal files, and give copies to the people you designate to make such decisions.

Check your beneficiaries. Regardless of what your will specifies, your life insurance, your IRAs, pension, and your other retirement accounts will go to the person listed as a beneficiary on file with the insurance company or IRA administrator. To update them, call the customer service line for your insurer or your IRA or 401(k) and fill out a new form; you may be able to update these online.

Then, every few years—such as every presidential election year or every Winter Olympics year—check them and ensure they're up to date.

Other questions. Once the big legal issues are up to date, you should take care of personal matters as well. Remember that big list of accounts that had to be changed back in Chapter 1? If something happened to you, how would your children, parents, or siblings know what bank or credit card accounts you have, what kinds of insurance you have, your cell-phone service provider, or other key bills or benefits?

After going through all this yourself, you hopefully will be motivated to create a list of all your relevant financial accounts, putting it in a sealed envelope in a file or a drawer that would be accessible in an emergency. The list should also include contact information for your financial planner, accountant, lawyer, insurance agent, benefits department, and, if you have your own business, any key business contacts. In addition, consider including a list of your user names and passwords so that your trusted power of attorney could have online access. You should let the person who will have your power of attorney know where to find the information if it is needed.

In addition, let your immediate family know your personal desires about the end of life: Would you like a funeral or memorial service and if so, do you have specific wishes for it? Would you like to be cremated or buried, and if buried, where? Do you want to be an organ donor? Would you like memorial donations to go to specific charities, and if so, which ones? Do you have any other specific wishes?

Once you have taken care of these documents and questions and let the important people in your life know about them, you can put them away for a while. But people move and age, and other situations change, so it's a good idea to update them along with your beneficiaries, perhaps every presidential election year.

As grim and tedious as this process is, it's one of the kindest and most valuable things you can do for your own family, easing them into their own fresh start.

At this point, your journey has been a challenging one, and you may feel like you still have a way to go emotionally. In time, you can put some setbacks behind you, while some difficult losses stay with you forever. But even as you continue to work through your situation, you should feel empowered by the skills you now have in understanding and managing your money and planning for your financial future. You know how to budget, how to save and invest, and how to get your financial life in tip-top shape. You know what questions to ask, where to get help, and how to continue your journey. The road ahead may still have its bumps, but you're well on your way to a new financial life.

HELPFUL WEBSITES

The Internet is a wonderful place for finding quick answers, but it is also full of dated, inaccurate, or even misleading information. These sites should help give you a head start in finding the information that you need.

This is far from a comprehensive list, however, and the listings below aren't an endorsement of any sites. Be aware that some of these, such as the banking and credit card sites, make money by promoting certain products and won't offer a comprehensive list of offerings. You may do just as well or better by going to a local bank or a credit union.

Many local newspapers list mortgages rates, CD and savings rates, and other local information once a week. You can also find information about most personal finance subjects at WSJ.com, SmartMoney.com, and MarketWatch.com.

ADVISERS
Where to find them and where to check them out
www.AdvisorInfo.SEC.gov, to check out your financial adviser
    with the SEC
www.CFP.net/search/, the Certified Financial Planner Board
    of Standards
www.FindLegalHelp.org, the American Bar Association lawyer
    referral site
www.FINRA.org/brokercheck/, to check out your broker

www.FPAnet.org, the Financial Planning Association

www.Martindale.com, the Martindale-Hubbell site for looking up lawyers' work

www.NAPFA.org, the National Association of Personal Financial Advisors

public.findlaw.com/library/hiring-lawyer/state-attorney -discipline-links.html, link to state groups that discipline lawyers

Budgeting and Debt Help

www.CCCServices.com, Consumer Credit Counseling Services

www.justice.gov/ust/eo/bapcpa/ccde/cc_approved.htm, the government site for finding authorized nonprofit credit-counseling services

www.Mint.com, online budgeting software

www.NFCC.org, National Foundation for Credit Counseling, a site for finding nonprofit credit-counseling services

http://online.wsj.com/public/page/booktools.html, a simple budgeting tool

Car Buying

Information about cars, reviews, car prices, negotiating suggestions, and other tips

www.Autos.yahoo.com, Yahoo!'s car site

www.CarFax.com, service that will check a used vehicle's history

www.Cars.com, broad car site

www.CarTalk.com, the site of the popular public radio show

www.ConsumerReports.org, well-known for its thorough car testing, requires subscription

www.Edmunds.com, a top site for seeing what others are paying for new cars

www.IIHS.org/ratings/, the Insurance Institute for Highway Safety car crash ratings

www.JDPower.com, also known for its testing

www.KBB.com (for Kelley Blue Book), a top site for car pricing www.NADA.com, the National Association of Auto Dealers

www.SaferCar.gov, the U.S. government's auto-crash ratings

College Savings, Student Loans, and Financial Aid

www.CollegeAnswer.com, the education site for a large student-loan lender

www.CollegeBoard.com, look for the Pay for College section

www.College.gov, a government site

www.FAFSA.gov, the site for the crucial financial-aid form

www.FastWeb.com, comprehensive scholarship information

www.FinAid.org, a very comprehensive financial-aid site

www.LoanConsolidation.ed.gov, the government site for student-loan consolidation

www.PrivateCollege529.com, a savings plan for those who expect to go to private colleges

www.SavingforCollege.com, a comprehensive site on 529 plans

www.StudentAid.ed.gov, a government site for financial aid

Credit Cards

Where to compare terms, interest rates, and special offers

www.BillShrink.com, a site for comparing credit card rates, television and cell phone services, and other consumer services

www.CardHub.com

www.CardRatings.com

www.CreditCards.com

www.Credit.com, site with advice and card insight

www.FederalReserve.gov/Pubs/shop/ (Federal Reserve information on choosing a card)

www.NerdWallet.com

Credit Reports and Scores

Where to get your credit report and your credit score

www.AnnualCreditReport.com, the site for getting your free credit report from the big three credit reporting services

www.Equifax.com, a credit-reporting service

www.Experian.com, a credit-reporting service

www.MyFico.com, the consumer site from Fair Isaac, creator of the FICO score. The forums on this site are especially informative

www.Transunion.com, a credit-reporting service

INSURANCE INFORMATION

Where to find out more about insurance

www.AccuCoverage.com, homeowners insurance site

www.AccuQuote.com, an insurance shopping site

http://eapps.naic.org/cis/, site for checking whether an insurance company has received more or fewer consumer complaints than average

www.eHealthInsurance.com, health-insurance shopping site

www.FloodSmart.gov, the US government's flood insurance site

www.HealthCare.gov, the government's health insurance site

www.HealthCompare.com, health-insurance shopping site

www.III.org, site of the Insurance Information Institute, a group supported by the insurance industry

www.Insure.com, an insurance shopping site

www.InsWeb.com, auto-insurance shopping site

www.knowyourstuff.org, home inventory software

www.LifeHappens.org, a life-insurance education site with calculators

www.naic.org, site of the National Association of Insurance Commissioners

INVESTING INFORMATION

Sources for more specific information on various
kinds of investments

Apps.finra.org/fundanalyzer/1/fa.aspx, the Financial Industry Regulatory Authority's analyzer for mutual funds and exchange traded funds and their expenses

www.FINRA.org/InvestorInformation/ToolsCalculators/index.htm, FINRA calculators

www.ICI.org/funds, an investor section of the Investment

Company Institute, the mutual-fund industry's trade group, which has many links to other financial sites

www.IndexUniverse.com, for ETF information

www.LipperLeaders.com, a good site for researching mutual funds

www.Morningstar.com, a top site for researching mutual funds and stocks and comparing fund costs. Using some of the best services requires a subscription

www.NASAA.org, the trade group for state security regulators, the North American Securities Administrators Association

www.TreasuryDirect.gov, the U.S. Treasury's site for buying government notes and bonds directly

LOAN AND INTEREST RATES

Where to find the rates for mortgages and auto loans
www.BankRate.com
www.Google.com/advisor/
www.HSH.com

MORTGAGE AND HOME-BUYING ISSUES

Where to find information on buying a home, renting, or resolving mortgage woes
www.GinnieMae.gov/ypth/, Ginnie Mae buy vs. rent calculator

www.HopeNow.com, a site for an alliance of credit counselors and mortgage companies

www.KnowYourOptions.com, Fannie Mae's site for helping with troubled mortgages

www.MakingHomeAffordable.gov, a government site for helping with troubled mortgages

www.realtor.com/home-finance/

SAVINGS RATES

Where to find the best interest rates on CDs, money market accounts, and money market mutual funds
www.BankRate.com

www.DepositAccounts.com

www.Google.com/advisor/

www.iMoneyNet.com, money market mutual fund rates

Social Security Benefits

http://ssa.gov/onlineservices/, site that links to online applications

www.ssa.gov/survivorplan/index.htm, information about Social Security benefits for widows/widowers and their children

Taxes

Where to find the basics

www.Fool.com/taxes, articles on lots of tax issues

www.IRS.gov, the Internal Revenue Service site; search by topic

Wills and Estates

Where to find help with end-of-life issues

www.AgingWithDignity.org, home of a Five Wishes document to guide your family if you can't make decisions yourself

www.Caringinfo.org, site with links to state-specific living wills and advance directives

www.LegalZoom.com, will-making and other legal software

www.Nolo.com, will-making and other legal software

GLOSSARY

Adjustable Rate Mortgage (ARM): A mortgage where the interest rate starts at a low teaser rate, but then adjusts every year (or at another specified time), based on movements in a particular index. If rates in the economy go up, your rate—and your mortgage payment—can climb dramatically over time.

Adjusted Gross Income (AGI): A calculation for income tax purposes that reflects your income, including your paycheck, dividends, and interest, minus certain expenses, such as IRA contributions or alimony payments.

Advance Health Care Directive: Sometimes called an Advance Health Directive, this document or documents (depending on your state laws) let your family and doctor know your health-care preferences in case you aren't in the physical or emotional shape to make them. These include designating who can make decisions for you if you are in an accident or incapacitated and might include your feelings about prolonging your life or whether you want to be an organ donor. A "Living Will" is a form of advance health directive.

Amortization Schedule: A breakdown of the interest and principal paid with each payment on an installment loan. Initially, most of the payment goes to interest. By the end of the loan's term, most of the payment goes to principal.

Annual Percentage Rate (APR): The bottom-line interest rate charged on debt-like credit cards and loans, allowing you to compare one offer to another. This number uses a standardized computation to take into account fees and costs and give you an actual annualized cost.

Annual Percentage Yield (APY): The interest paid over a full year's time on products such as bank accounts and certificates of deposits, allowing you to compare various offerings. The APY uses a standardized computation to take into account the effect of compounding, or the interest paid on your interest earned during the year.

Appreciation: An increase in value or price over time.

Assets: Items of value that can be converted into cash.

Back-end Load: A sales charge applied when you sell shares of certain mutual funds.

Bankruptcy: The last-resort legal process for working out your debts. Under Chapter 7 bankruptcy, individuals ask a judge to wipe out or discharge most of their debts; under Chapter 13, individuals put together a plan to repay all or part of their debts. Some debts, such as taxes, child support, alimony, and student loans typically aren't discharged.

Basis Point: 1/100 of a percentage point. An increase of a quarter of a percentage point is the same as an increase of 25 basis points.

Bear Market: A stock market when prices are generally falling. Some investment professionals define a bear market as one in which a broad measure of stocks, such as the Dow Jones Industrial Average, declines at least 20 percent.

Beneficiary: A person or entity designated to receive property or other assets from a will, retirement account, or insurance policy.

Big Board: Nickname for the New York Stock Exchange.

Bonds: Debt issued by companies or governments with a promise to repay the original amount plus specified interest by a certain date. Most bonds are issued in increments of $1,000 face value.

Bond Ladder: A method of reducing your risk and increasing your yield with bond investments by buying bonds that mature in intervals. A bond ladder might include a bond that matures in two years, one that matures in four years, one in six years, and one in eight years. When the first bond matures, it is replaced with a bond maturing in eight years, continuing the ladder.

Broker: A person or company that acts as a middleman in a transaction, helping you buy or sell stocks, real estate, or insurance in exchange for a commission or fee.

Bull Market: A stock market when prices are generally rising.

Capital Gains and Losses: A gain or loss on the sale of an asset like stock or real estate bought as an investment. The Internal Revenue Service taxes capital gains on many assets held for at least a year at a lower rate than regular income or short-term gains to encourage long-term investment and entrepreneurship.

Cash Advance: Borrowing on your credit card to get cash. The credit card company will charge you a fee for using your credit card for a cash withdrawal and will charge interest until the advance is paid back. This is an expensive way to get cash that should be used only in emergency situations.

Certificate of Deposit: A type of account that pays a fixed interest rate if you agree to leave your money alone for a certain period of time. These are issued by banks and insured by the Federal Deposit Insurance Corporation for up to $250,000. You can buy CDs with maturities from one month to five years or longer. However, if you need your money before the CD matures, you will pay a penalty for withdrawing it.

COBRA: The Consolidated Omnibus Budget Reconciliation Act gives workers and their families the right to pay to extend their health insurance for a period of time after a job loss, death, divorce, or other life events. While they maintain their health-care benefits, individuals typically pay more for health insurance under COBRA than they paid to their employer because they bear the full cost of the premium.

Comprehensive: In car insurance, coverage of damage to your own car. In health insurance, a plan that covers everything, including hospitalization and doctor visits.

Co-payment: The portion of a medical bill that the insurance company requires you to pay when you visit the doctor. Also called the co-pay.

Coupon Rate: In a bond, this is the interest rate paid each year. A bond with a coupon of 5 percent pays $50 in interest for each $1,000 of face value, usually in two installments.

Credit Limit: The maximum amount you can borrow on your credit card. Under the Credit Card Act of 2009, you must formally agree to pay an over-limit fee if you want to be able to exceed your credit limit.

Credit Score: A numerical grade that aims to tell lenders how likely you are to repay your debts. Your credit score is based on your past payment record, how much you borrow, how long you've been borrowing, and other factors. The best known is the FICO score developed by Fair Isaac Corporation.

Debit Card: A card that looks like a credit card but works more like a personal check. When you use a debit card, whether to withdraw money from an ATM or make purchases, the funds are withdrawn from your bank account right away. When you make a purchase, you can either put in your PIN, or personal identification number, or sign a receipt as you would with a credit card. Debit cards can be more convenient than using cash, but they have fewer protections than credit cards.

Deductible: In insurance, the amount you must pay before your insurance kicks in. For instance, if your car sustains $2,000 in damage and your deductible is $500, you will pay $500 and the insurance company will pay $1,500. With health insurance, you must meet the deductible each year before insurance will pay its part; with car, homeowners, or renters insurance, the deductible applies to each claim you make. Generally, the higher the deductible you're willing to pay, the less your insurance will cost.

Deductions: Items that help reduce the federal income tax you owe by reducing your taxable income. Depending on their size and your income, mortgage interest, charitable contributions, and property taxes can be tax deductions that trim the income taxes you pay.

Default: A failure to pay a debt. The terms of the debt determine how long the debt must be overdue before it is considered to be in default.

Dependent Care Account: An opportunity for working parents to put away pre-tax dollars toward child care for youngsters under thirteen years old. Offered through employers, these plans allow you to put up to $5,000 per family a year into an account before taxes and then use the funds to pay for day care centers, nannies, or day camps.

Diversification: Investing in a mix of stocks and bonds to reduce your risk while maintaining or improving your return. Rather than putting all your eggs in one basket, diversification helps minimize the ups and downs of investing.

Dollar-cost Averaging: The process of investing regularly in the stock market, such as every month or every quarter, regardless of the price. Dollar-cost averaging smoothes out the highs and lows and eliminates worries about buying at a high point.

Dow Jones Industrial Average (DJIA): An average of thirty industrial stocks that serves as a representation of the broader stock market. When the guy on TV says the market was up or down, he is usually referring to the performance of the Dow Jones average that day.

Down Payment: An initial cash payment on a large purchase. With a car or home, the rest of the amount owed is usually financed through a loan that is repaid over time.

Earnings per Share: How much profit a company earns for each share of stock it has outstanding. The earnings per share is calculated by dividing the quarterly or annual net income by the number of outstanding shares.

Equity: Ownership. In real estate, your equity is the portion of the property that is yours after the debt is subtracted. If you own a $400,000 home with a $300,000 mortgage, your equity is $100,000. In investing, stocks are often called "equities."

Escrow: Money or property put into the hands of a third party until certain conditions are met. For instance, when you make a deposit on a property purchase, your initial deposit may be held in escrow until you close the deal. In addition, your mortgage company may collect monthly payments on property taxes and homeowners insurance and hold on to them until those payments are due.

Estate: All the things you own that have value. Estate planning refers to planning for how your assets will be distributed at your death.

Exchange-traded Fund (ETF): A type of investment that acts like a mutual fund but can be bought and sold like a stock. Exchange-traded funds often mimic an index like the Standard & Poor's 500. But unlike an index mutual fund, the price fluctuates during the day and the ETF can be bought and sold at any time and there is no minimum purchase required.

Expense Ratio: A mutual fund's annual operating costs, stated as a percentage of its assets. Operating expenses are subtracted from fund assets and reduce the investment returns earned by fund shareholders.

Face Value: In bonds, the amount of the original bond and the amount paid when the bond comes due, usually $1,000. The face value is also known as the "par value."

FICO Score: A credit score developed by Fair Isaac Corporation, ranging from 300 to 850, based on your debt, payment history, and other factors that is intended to measure how likely you are to repay a loan. Lenders look to this score to assess how risky it would be to loan money to you.

Fiduciary: A person who manages assets for the benefit of someone else and who is required to put that person's interests above his or her own. Real estate brokers have a fiduciary duty to the seller of a property, but often not to the buyer. Some financial advisers act as fiduciaries and others do not.

Fixed-income Investments: Investments that return income at regular, fixed intervals, like savings accounts, certificates of deposits, and bonds.

Fixed-rate Mortgage: A home loan with an interest rate and monthly payment that will stay the same over the life of the loan. Most fixed-rate mortgages are for either thirty-year or fifteen-year terms.

Flexible Spending Account: A work benefit that allows you to use pre-tax income to help pay for child care or medical expenses. Once a year, your employer will give you the opportunity to determine how much you want to contribute to this account before income taxes, Social Security, and Medicare, up to certain maximums. These accounts have a use-it-or-lose-it feature. If you don't spend all that you put away over a calendar year (and, sometimes, a short grace period after the year ends), you will lose the money.

Foreclosure: The process where a bank or other lender takes possession of a home after the homeowner has failed to keep up with mortgage or home-equity loan payments. The lender can then sell the home to someone else to recoup all or part of the loan.

Formulary: A list of prescription medicines compiled by your health insurance company detailing what medicines are covered under the plan and at what rates.

401(k) Plan: Named for the provision of the tax code that allowed retirement contributions to be made before taxes, these company-sponsored plans allow you to make pre-tax contributions toward your retirement and allow the investments to grow tax-deferred until you reach retirement age. If you withdraw your investments early, you will pay income taxes on the amount plus a 10 percent tax penalty. When you withdraw the money during retirement, the funds will be taxed as income.

Free Application for Federal Student Aid (FAFSA): The form that students and parents need to fill out if the student is interested in need-based financial aid for college.

Front-end Load: An up-front sales charge applied when you buy shares of certain mutual funds.

Growth Stocks: Stocks of companies whose profits are expected to grow much faster than average. Buyers hope that growth will translate into above-average increases in the stock price.

Health Savings Account: An account designed to help those with health-care plans that have high deductibles. You can contribute pre-tax dollars to this account, and money in the account can grow tax-free. The funds can be used to pay for medical expenses. Unlike a flexible spending account, these funds can be carried over year to year and can be invested.

Index Mutual Fund: A mutual fund that tracks a specific stock or bond index, such as the Standard & Poor's 500 stock index of five hundred large stocks. Typically, these funds have lower expenses than funds that are actively managed.

Individual Retirement Account (IRA): Tax-favored accounts for retirement savings that you establish outside of your employer. Individuals who don't have other retirement plans or who meet income requirements can make tax-deductible contributions to these accounts, which grow tax-deferred. *See also* Roth IRA.

Interest Rate: The annual percentage to be paid on the amount originally borrowed. A savings account may pay from less than 1 percent to 5 percent interest per year, or less than $1 to $5 for each $100 saved. A credit card may charge 17 percent or more interest a year on your balances, or $17 or more for each $100 owed.

Intestate: A person who dies without a legal will. State laws spell out how assets are distributed in these situations.

Itemizing Deductions: If your total tax deductions are greater than the standard deduction allowed by the Internal Revenue Service, you can itemize or list them on Form 1040. Itemizing deductions can reduce your overall income tax bill.

Jumbo Mortgage: A mortgage loan above a certain limit. In 2011, that was $417,000 in most markets, but it could be as much as 50 percent higher in expensive areas, such as New York City or Los Angeles. Generally, the interest rates on jumbo loans are slightly more costly than for conventional mortgages.

Junk Bond: A bond that is considered too risky to be investment grade. Bonds rated BB or lower by Standard & Poor's or Ba or lower by Moody's are considered to be speculative or "junk" bonds.

Keogh Plan: A type of retirement plan for self-employed people or entities that aren't incorporated.

Large-cap Stock: Generally speaking, a company with a market capitalization—or a stock market value—of $10 billion or more.

Liabilities: Debts and other financial obligations. The opposite of assets.

Life-cycle Funds: Diversified mutual funds that may own stocks, bonds, and cash in a mix aimed at the long term. The funds typically aim toward a specific retirement date. These funds are intended to give investors one simple option for retirement investing.

Liquidity: The ability to pay your bills with cash on hand or to convert your assets to cash quickly. Because most stocks trade daily, they are very liquid; investments in art or real estate, however, are less liquid because they can be difficult and time-consuming to sell.

Market Cap: A company's stock-market value, measured by multiplying its stock price times the number of shares it has outstanding. Market cap is short for *market capitalization.*

Maturity: When a security such as a bond comes due or is to be paid in full.

Mid-cap Stock: Generally speaking, a company with a market capitalization—or a stock market value—of $2 billion to $10 billion.

Money Market Account: A kind of savings account typically offered by banks and credit unions. Money market accounts often pay higher interest rates than regular saving accounts, but also require larger balances. They are insured up to $250,000.

Money Market Mutual Fund: A mutual fund that invests in very short-term, highly liquid securities and aims to maintain a constant price of $1 a share. Money market mutual funds are not insured but are considered low risk.

Mortgage: A home loan or other real estate loan.

Municipal Bonds: Debt issued by a state, county, or local govern-ment. Also known as "munis." Interest is usually exempt from federal income tax and also from state tax in the state where it was issued.

Mutual Fund: A professionally managed pool of money funded by a number of investors. Mutual fund managers may buy stocks, bonds, or other securities based on the fund's goals and objectives for the benefit of the whole group.

Nasdaq Stock Market: An electronic stock market that is home to many technology stocks. The acronym once stood for the National Association of Securities Dealers Automated Quota-tion. Stocks traded on the Nasdaq often have ticker symbols with four letters.

Net Worth: Your assets, including all your investments, bank ac-counts, and items of value, minus your liabilities, including your debts.

Network Health Care: Doctors, hospitals, and other health-care providers that have signed contracts with your health insurance company to provide services at certain prices. Generally, your insurance company will reimburse you more for in-network providers than for those that aren't part of its network.

New York Stock Exchange: The oldest and most prestigious stock exchange in the United States, sometimes called the Big Board. Stocks traded on the NYSE usually have three-letter ticker symbols, though a select few go by one letter.

No-load Fund: A mutual fund without a commission or sales charge.

Out-of-pocket Maximum: In health insurance, this is the maxi-mum amount you'll have to pay for health care in a given year (not including your monthly premiums). After you have paid deductibles, co-pays, and your portion of medical expenses up to your out-of-pocket maximum, your health insurance should pick up the rest of the bills.

Overdraft: When you write checks or make payments with your debit card that exceed the amount of money in your account, resulting in a negative balance. Also known as bouncing a check. When this happens, your account is *overdrawn* and the bank has the option to pay or not pay the amount. If it does pay, it will probably charge you fees that must be paid in addition to repaying the overdraft amount. You may also have to pay fees to the store that got the bounced check.

Overdraft Protection: A bank service where the bank agrees to loan you the money to cover your overdrafts up to a certain amount. In order to get overdraft protection, you must opt in or agree to it. You can also link your savings account or a credit card to your checking account so that funds are taken from one of those if you overdraw your account. You'll still pay fees, but they likely will be smaller than overdraft fees.

Par Value: The face value of a bond, usually $1,000.

Personal Identification Number (PIN): Your personal secret password that gives you access to ATMs, online accounts, and other password-protected accounts.

Phishing: Using a fake website, pop-up advertisement, or e-mail that looks legitimate to extract personal information or account information from unsuspecting victims.

Points: In home-buying, one point equals 1 percent of the amount borrowed. Points are up-front fees assessed to lower your mortgage interest rate or fees required to close the loan. In bond prices, a point is 1 percent of the bond's face value, or

$10 for every $1,000 face value. In stocks, a point is $1; a stock that's up three points is up $3.

Portfolio: Your holdings of stocks, bonds, and other investments. A diversified portfolio will have a mix of investments.

Preexisting Condition: A medical ailment that existed before you signed up for your health insurance. Some policies may exclude coverage of preexisting conditions for a period of time. The new health-care law prevents companies from excluding the preexisting conditions of children, a provision that will be extended to adults in 2014.

Preferred Stock: A kind of stock that typically pays a fixed dividend. Preferred shares tend to trade based on their dividend yield, more like a bond. But unlike a bond, preferred stock doesn't come with a maturity date. Companies must pay the dividend on preferred shares before they pay dividends on common shares.

Premium: In insurance, the amount you pay the insurance company for your coverage. Premiums may be paid monthly, once a year, or on different payment schedules. With bonds, a premium is the amount you pay for the bond above the face value. When current interest rates are lower than a bond's coupon rate, the bond may trade at a premium to its face value.

Price-to-Earnings Ratio (P/E Ratio): A measure of how a stock is valued by the market. The P/E ratio reflects how much investors are willing to pay for each $1 of company profits. The P/E is calculated by dividing a company's current stock price by its most recent four quarters of earnings per share. A *forward P/E* is calculated by dividing the current stock price by the expected earnings per share over the next year.

Primary Care Physician (PCP): Your main doctor, who acts as the point person for health insurance purposes. Some health insurance plans require you to see your primary care physician first or to get a referral from that doctor before you can see a specialist.

Principal: In a loan, the actual amount you borrowed. With an installment loan like a mortgage, your regular payment covers primarily interest charges at the beginning and primarily the principal at the end.

Prospectus: A legal document that spells out the terms of a security being sold to the public. The prospectus should give you enough relevant information to make an informed decision.

Quote: The most recent price for a stock or bond. Also known as the *quoted price.*

Rebalancing: The process of periodically transferring money within your portfolio, say from stocks to bonds, so that it meets your asset-allocation goals. Because one sector of the market may outperform another, you may want to bring your portfolio back into balance once or twice a year by rebalancing your investment mix.

Replacement Cost Coverage: Insurance coverage that will pay you enough to actually replace possessions that have been damaged or destroyed, rather than reimbursing you based on their recent market price.

Roth 401(k): An employer-sponsored retirement savings account funded with after-tax money. Once invested, the funds can grow tax-free and are tax-free when they are withdrawn at retirement. This investment makes sense for people who think they may be in a higher tax bracket in retirement than they are now.

Roth Individual Retirement Account (Roth IRA): A kind of retirement account funded with after-tax dollars that then grow tax-free. Withdrawals at retirement are also tax-free. The contributions can be withdrawn tax-free at any time.

Rule of 72: The mathematical rule that helps you figure out when you will double your money by dividing your expected interest rate or return into 72. For example, investments with an average return of 8 percent will double every nine years. To figure out the return you need to double your money in a certain time period, divide the time period into 72.

Russell 2000 Index: An index of two thousand small-company stocks. The Russell 2000 is a widely followed benchmark for the small-cap company universe.

Secured Credit Card: A credit card backed by a deposit in a bank account. The available credit on the card is limited by the amount in the account. Secured cards are designed for people with no credit record or a poor one and can help those individuals rebuild or establish a credit history.

Short-selling: A bet that a stock price will go down. Short sellers borrow stock from brokerage firms and sell it, with the goal of buying back at a lower price.

Simplified Employee Pension (SEP-IRA): A kind of retirement plan for the self-employed and for those at companies without retirement plans. Contributions to a SEP-IRA are tax-deductible. Investments grow tax-deferred and you will pay taxes when you withdraw the funds at retirement.

Small-cap Stock: Generally speaking, a company with a market capitalization—or a stock market value—of between $300 million and $2 billion.

Social Security: The government program that provides retirement and disability income.

Standard & Poor's 500 Stock Index: An index of five hundred large-cap US stocks that is considered a benchmark for the stock market.

Standard Deduction: A deduction available to all taxpayers that reduces the amount on which you pay federal income taxes. The size of the deduction depends on whether you are married and how many people are in your household, among other things. The standard deduction applies only to people who don't itemize their tax deductions.

Stock: A kind of security that reflects ownership in a company. Also called equity or shares. Over time, stock ownership has outperformed other investments.

Stock Option: The right to buy a stock at a specific price up to a certain date. Companies issue stock options as a way to compensate executives and others and as a way to encourage managers and employees to think like stockholders.

Strike Price: The price at which a stock option can be exercised. Also called the exercise price. If your company grants you options to buy a hundred shares at $50 a share, then your strike price is $50. You would exercise the option only if the current price is above the strike price.

Target Date Mutual Fund: A mutual fund that is structured with a specific retirement date in mind, such as a 2050 fund. The fund will own a mix of stocks, bonds, and cash and will be more aggressive in the early years and more conservative as the target date draws near. Also known as *life-cycle* funds.

Tax Deferral: A delay in taxation until funds are actually withdrawn. Then, the withdrawals are taxed. Individual retirement accounts and 401(k)s grow tax-deferred, but are taxed when the retiree taps them.

Tax-Free: Not subject to current or future tax consequences. Contributions to Roth IRAs are made after taxes, and both the growth and the withdrawals are tax-free. The interest on municipal bonds is generally free from federal income tax and from state taxes in the state where they are issued.

Teaser Rate: An initial, temporary rate intended to entice you to sign up for a credit card or other loan or to open an interest-bearing account. Typically, the rate changes after three or six months to one that's less attractive.

1040: One of the primary forms for filing federal income taxes. Some taxpayers can file using the simpler 1040EZ or 1040A.

Term Life Insurance: Pure life insurance that provides coverage over a set period of time. When the policy is up, you have a choice of renewing it or letting it lapse. By contrast, *cash value life insurance* has an investment component as well as a life insurance piece.

Treasurys: Securities sold by the US Treasury to meet government expenses. Treasury bills mature within one year, Treasury notes mature within one to ten years, and Treasury bonds mature in more than ten years. Treasury notes and bonds are sold in denominations of $100 and pay interest twice a year.

Underwater or Upside Down: Terms used to describe a situation where you owe more on something than it is now worth. If your home price drops below what you owe on your mortgage or your car loan is for more than the value of your car, you are said to be underwater or upside down.

Value Stock: A stock believed to have greater potential than its current price indicates. Investors see value stocks as bargains that are undervalued relative to their real worth.

Variable Interest Rate: An interest rate that changes with moves in interest rate benchmarks, such as the US prime rate or the LIBOR, the London Interbank Offer Rate.

Vesting: The process under which employees receive benefits over a period of time. Stock options that are granted typically vest over three or four years; a three-year vesting period means you'll take ownership of one-third the first year, two-thirds the second year, and all of them the third year. Companies may require five or more years of service before you are vested in a pension plan. Some matches in 401(k) plans vest over one to six years.

W-2 Form: The form your employer sends to you and the IRS every year showing what you earned and how much was withheld for taxes.

W-4 Form: The form you fill out when you start a job that determines how much of your pay is withheld for income taxes. You can file a new W-4 to increase or decrease your withholding at any time.

Withholding: Taxes taken out from each paycheck.

Yield: The percentage return on an investment or loan. A $100 investment that pays $5 a year in interest has a yield of 5 percent. Financial companies use standard methods in quoting the yields on bank accounts, money market funds, and bonds.

Yield to Maturity: The annual yield, or percentage return, received if you hold a bond until it matures. The yield to maturity is one of the most widely quoted yields for bonds.

ACKNOWLEDGMENTS

Special thanks go to the following people for graciously sharing their insights and expertise:

Eleanor Blayney, Directions for Women; Don Linzer, Schneider Downs; June Walbert, USAA; Barry Paperno, FICO; Ken Lin, CreditKarma.com; John Ulzheimer, SmartCredit .com; Tom Pamperin, Veterans Affairs; Bruce McClary, Sam Hussain, Sandra Brown, and Ashley Adami, all of Clearpoint Financial Solutions; Susan Seiter, 1st Global; Teal Thawley, Nolan Shaw, Michelle Manners, and Mark Cason.

Rose Ellen D'Angelo at *The Wall Street Journal* once again provided amazing support from start to finish. Karen Damato backed me up with her eagle eye and encyclopedic knowledge. Talia Krohn at Crown Business was an extremely patient and thoughtful editor.

I am especially grateful and indebted to my husband, Scott McCartney, who read drafts early and often, put up with the long hours, and was always there for me.

INDEX

ABOUT THE AUTHOR

KAREN BLUMENTHAL writes the "Getting Going" personal finance column for *The Wall Street Journal* and has been a financial journalist for more than twenty-five years.

She has written about a wide range of financial and corporate subjects and is the author of *The Wall Street Journal Guide to Starting Your Financial Life* and *Grande Expectations: A Year in the Life of Starbucks' Stock.* She has also written four nonfiction books for young people.

As an author, she has appeared on the *Today Show,* CNBC, ABC's *World News Tonight,* and the PBS *Nightly Business Report.* She lives in Dallas.

978-0-307-46127-8
$14.99 paper (Canada: $16.99)

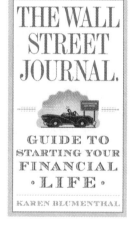

978-0-307-40708-5
$14.95 paper (Canada: $16.95)

978-0-307-40707-8
$14.95 paper (Canada: $17.50)

978-0-307-40893-8
$15.00 paper (Canada: $18.95)

978-0-307-40592-0
$14.95 paper (Canada: $16.95)

978-0-307-35099-2
$14.95 paper (Canada: $19.95)

978-0-307-35105-0
$15.95 paper (Canada: $19.95)

978-0-307-33853-2
$13.95 paper (Canada: $17.95)

978-0-307-33600-2
$14.95 paper (Canada: $21.00)

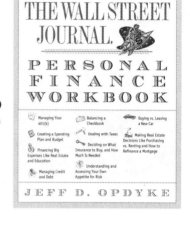

978-0-307-33601-9
$13.95 paper (Canada: $21.00)

978-0-307-34562-2
$14.95 paper (Canada: $21.00)

978-0-307-23699-9
$14.95 paper (Canada: $21.00)

Available wherever books are sold.